SCIENTIFIC AMERICAN

Building the Elite Athlete

The Editors of *Scientific American*

THE LYONS PRESS
Guilford, Connecticut
An Imprint of The Globe Pequot Press

The Lyons Press is an imprint of The Globe Pequot Press

10 9 8 7 6 5 4 3 2 1

Printed in the United States of America

Edited by David L. Green
Designed by Casey Shain

Library of Congress Cataloging-in-Publication Data

Scientific American building the elite athlete / by the editors of Scientific American.
     p. cm.
  Includes index.
  ISBN 978-1-59921-116-9
  1. Sports sciences. I. Scientific American. II. Title: Building the elite athlete.
  GV558.S35 2007
  613.7'1--dc22

                                                                    2007008908

CONTENTS

INTRODUCTION

Game Theory

GARY STIX AND MARK FISCHETTI

At the ancient Olympics, the Greeks practiced the long jump. But no one really knew how long anyone jumped. Exact distance was a sketchy notion. As sports historian Allen Guttman notes, a unit of length in Sparta differed from one in Athens. Comparison of performances from one competition to the next was impossible and bore no interest anyway to the sponsors of what were mostly religious and ritualistic events.

It wasn't until a few millennia later that modern sport made its debut, characterized by precise quantification of distance and time. The machine age began an era of standardization in sport, which prompted rules and regulations, timepieces, set-length playing fields, scoring systems and sophisticated equipment.

This rationalism was gradually applied to improving an athlete's body and skill. Physical conditioning has ancient roots in the Greek and Roman desire to develop superior soldiery. But a rigorously scientific approach to *citius, altius, fortius*—the Olympic motto of swifter, higher, stronger—only came in the 20th century.

Today the burgeoning base of scientific and technical knowledge in industrialized countries has channeled enormous effort into transforming sport into science that goes beyond traditional trial and error methodology.

To provide the elite athlete with that critical edge, scientists and technologists are now trying to define athletic performance as a set of physical parameters (such as force vectors and acceleration), biological processes (pulse rate and maximum oxygen uptake) and mental states (psyched up or psyched out).

Physiologists, kinesiologists, nutritionists, biomechanists and psychologists (and sometimes even coaches) are exploring whether they can translate fundamental insights from physics and biology into practical training technique. Is there a "perfect" swimming stroke that can create the hundredths-of-a-second advantage that distinguishes a winner from an also swam? Can skateboarders, snowboarders, gymnasts and divers perform even more complex maneuvers with a better understanding of how to exploit the physics of twisting bodies?

Engineers have crafted technology to aid athletes as well—sometimes threatening the very integrity of a sport. Advances in golf balls, javelins, speed skates and tennis rackets have so improved performance that occasionally they have had to be regulated or banned so as not to undermine the fundamental human challenge that defines a game. Technology is supplementing the human judgment of referees, too. And it has fostered extreme sports such as deep underwater diving, extreme skiing and base jumping (from skyscrapers or cliffs) and other pursuits that induce the mental rush of cheating death.

The importance that society accords to ensuring the health and welfare of a linebacker or point guard has spurred a concurrent boom in sports medicine. This discipline has become more than the domain of the superstar professional as the obsession with sport and fitness extends to all reaches of society. And the huge influx of women has prompted a long-overdue focus on the special types of injuries they experience.

A basic knowledge of the mysteries of how muscles work gives athletes and their trainers the insight to optimize workouts and recuperation periods. This understanding might even reach beyond the world of sports by furnishing the aged with techniques and compounds that could counter muscle loss.

In some realms, sports scientists may have already reached a point where they have bragging rights. New insights into fast-twitch muscle fiber and VO_2max, combined with the introduction of better gear, may help explain why almost every athletic record in the books continues to be broken. And this unceasing one-upmanship highlights a more profound scientific debate over whether we have begun to approach the limits of human performance in running, jumping and lifting.

All of this achievement, though, masks a stark reality. So far we have only attained an imperfect realization of sport as science. Logically, the search for the ultimate athlete would culminate in combing through human DNA for genes that can distinguish between the future Olympian and someone who will have a tough time making high school junior varsity. Genetic investigators have found a few tantalizing clues but mostly dead ends for what could pass as "performance genes." Coaches, too, are often at odds with a science that in some cases replaces one theory with another every few years. And sports psychology, which is supposed to keep the athlete locked into the mental game, may be less a system for training the mind than a sophisticated pep talk clothed in jargon.

Cynicism about the powers of positive thinking relates to the extent that any new record may be viewed not as a product of self-talk and personal grit, but rather as a success in concealing chemical enhancement. Illicit laboratories strive to concoct designer compounds that elude advanced sleuthing techniques, such as the carbon isotope ratio test to detect synthetic steroids, which have implicated champions like Justin Gatlin after he set a world record in the 100 meter dash and Floyd Landis after he took the 2006 Tour de France. Sadly, use of steroids by baseball sluggers and their alleged distribution by Balco, the Bay Area Laboratory Co-Operative supplements lab in California, smack of a long tradition promulgated by the former Soviet and East German sports institutes—which for a long time were considered the bellwethers of brilliant, dispassionate training but have since been revealed as little more than major dispensaries for anabolic steroids. Despite the tarnish, elite athletes are already inquiring how they can exploit an even more sophisticated cheat: gene doping, in which an injection of DNA would prod cells to increase production of muscle-building biochemicals.

Sports science has its contribution to make. As records keep falling and competition intensifies, it will become ever more difficult for an athlete to shave off that extra hundredth of a second or squeeze another millimeter of clearance over the bar in the unceasing quest to win a ticket to the top step on the winner's podium at the next Olympiad. Any leverage an athlete or coach can wrest from the wisdom of a Newton or the engineering wizardry of a Nike will be welcomed.

Scientific American Presents: Building the Elite Athlete, Fall 2000

Revised January 2007

CHAPTER 1

THE ATHLETE'S BODY

How Much Higher? How Much Faster?

Limits to human performance are not yet in sight

BRUCE SCHECHTER

Last year, during a rare stationary moment, runner Maurice Greene paused to reflect on world records. "You don't try to break them," he told a reporter. "You prepare the best you can, and they will come." A few weeks later in Athens, Greene's faith and preparation were rewarded when he set a new world record for the 100-meter dash, completing 45 precise and powerful strides in exactly 9.79 seconds. Greene had bested the previous record by five hundredths of a second—an eye blink, but also the single largest reduction in the past 30 years in this event, the ultimate sprint in track and field.

Can improvements in this and other sports go on? If athletes continue to refine their preparation, will world records continue to be the reward? Sports scientists and coaches wrestle with these questions on a daily basis. On the one hand, it is clear that there must be some limit to human performance: nobody who is still recognizably human will ever run faster than a speeding locomotive or leap tall buildings in a single bound. But so far no Einstein of the athletic universe has come along to set down the limits, although some have tried.

Ever since the early years of the 20th century, when the International Amateur Athletic Federation began keeping records, there has been a steady improvement in how fast athletes run, how high they jump and how far they are able to hurl massive objects of every description, themselves included, through space. For the so-called power events—those that, like the 100-meter sprint and the long jump, require a relatively brief, explosive release of energy—the times and distances have improved about 10 to 20 percent. In the endurance events the results have been even more dramatic. At the 1908 Olympics in London, John Hayes of the U.S. team ran a marathon in a time of 2:55:18. Last year Morocco's Khalid Khannouchi set a new world record of 2:05:42, almost 30 percent faster.

No one theory can explain such improvements in performance, but perhaps the most important factor has been genetics. "The athlete must choose his parents very carefully," says Jesus Dapena, a sports scientist at Indiana University, invoking an oft-cited adage. Over the past century the composition of the human gene pool has not changed appreciably; evolution operates on a far longer timescale. But with the increasing global participation in athletics—and ever greater rewards to tempt athletes—it is more likely that individuals possessing the unique complement of genes for athletic performance can be identified early. "Was there someone like [sprinter] Michael Johnson in the 1920s?" Dapena asks. "I'm sure there was, but he was probably a carpenter in the mountains."

Running on Genetics

Identifying genetically talented individuals is only the first step in creating world-class athletes. Michael Yessis, an emeritus professor of sports science at California State University at Fullerton, president of Sports Training in Escondido, Calif., as well as a consultant to many Olympic and professional teams, maintains that "genetics only determines about one third of an athlete's capabilities. But with the right training we can go much further with that one third than we've been going." Yessis believes that U.S. runners, despite their impressive achievements, are "running on their genetics." By applying more scientific methods, "they're going to go much faster." These methods include strength training that duplicates what they are doing in their running events as well as plyometrics, a technique pioneered in the former Soviet Union.

Whereas most exercises are designed to build up an athlete's strength or endurance, plyometrics focuses on increasing an athlete's power—that is, the rate at which she can expend energy. When a sprinter runs, Yessis explains, her foot stays in contact with the ground for only a little under a tenth of a second, half of which is devoted to landing and the other half to pushing off. Plyometric exercises help athletes make the best use of this brief interval.

Nutrition is another area that sports trainers have failed to address adequately. "Many athletes are not getting the best nutrition, even through supplements," Yessis insists. Each activity has its own particular nutritional needs. Few coaches, for instance, understand how deficiencies in trace minerals can lead to hamstring injuries.

Focused training will also play a role in enabling records to be broken. "If we would apply the Russian methods of training to some of the outstanding runners we have in this country," Yessis asserts, "they would be breaking records left and right." He will not predict by how much, however: "Exactly what the limits are it's hard to say. They're not going to be humongous, but there will be increases even if only by hundredths of a second. They will continue, as long as our methods continue to improve."

One of the most important new methodologies to be applied to sports training over the past several decades is known as biomechanics, the study of the body in motion. A biomechanic films an athlete in action and then digitizes her performance, recording the motion of every joint and limb in three dimensions. By applying Newton's laws to these motions, a biomechanic can determine what the athlete is doing to help her performance and what is holding her back. "We can say that this athlete's run is not fast enough; this one is not using his arms strongly enough during takeoff," says Dapena, who uses these methods to help high jumpers. Generally, the changes that a biomechanic can make in athletic performance are small. "We can't dismantle an athlete's technique," he notes. "We are just putting the icing on the cake."

To date, biomechanics has helped athletes only to fine-tune their techniques. Revolutionary ideas still come from the athletes themselves. "Normally athletes, by trial and error, come up with some crazy thing," Dapena explains. For example, during the 1968 Olympics in Mexico City, a relatively unknown high jumper named Dick Fosbury won the gold by going over the bar backward, in complete contradiction of all the received high-jumping wisdom, a move instantly dubbed the Fosbury flop.

The story of Fosbury's discovery illustrates the role of serendipity in advancing biomechanics. When Fosbury was growing up in Portland, Ore., he learned to jump over the high bar using the scissors kick—hopping over the bar with his rear end down— that was taught to children. In high school, his coach tried to convert him to the "correct" international style, which involved straddling the bar face down, in a forward roll. Fosbury, a gangly adolescent, found the technique difficult to master, so his coach allowed him to use the childish scissors in one meet. His first jump was an unimpressive 5 feet 4 inches. The problem, as he saw it, was that his rear kept knocking the bar. So he modified his approach to what he called "kind of a lazy scissors." As the bar moved higher, Fosbury found that he was beginning to go over flat on his back. "I'm upside down from everybody else," he recalled. "I go over at six feet, and nobody knows what the heck I'm doing."

Clearing the Higher Bar

Fosbury himself did not know what he was doing. That understanding took the later analysis of biomechanics specialists who put their minds to comprehending something that was too complex and unorthodox to have ever been invented through their own mathematical simulations. Even before Fosbury's strange jump, scientists had long known that when a high jumper leaps, his center of mass—the point at which the mass of a body appears to be concentrated—rises to a height determined by the energy generated by his muscles. Most of the time, when standing, sitting or running, our centers of mass are more or less within our bodies, so if we want our bodies to clear a bar, our center of mass must clear the bar as well.

Fosbury accidentally discovered that this is not always true: when the human body is arched backward, the center of mass can be made to move to just outside the back. In this position, a jumper's body can clear the bar while his center of mass travels beneath it. Thus, for the same energy expenditure, an athlete doing the Fosbury flop can clear a higher bar.

The inspiration provided by Fosbury also required another element that lies behind many improvements in athletic performance: an innovation in athletic equipment. In Fosbury's case, it was an improvement in the cushions that jumpers land on. Traditionally, high jumpers would land in pits filled with sawdust; flopping over the bar and landing backward in the pit would have been a recipe for injury. But by the time Fosbury was in high school, sawdust pits had been supplanted by large, soft foam cushions, ideal for flopping.

Other sports have benefited from better equipment. Speed skating was recently revolutionized when the Dutch introduced the "clap skate," a skate with a hinge that keeps the blade on the ice longer, providing more speed. Skaters were slow to adopt this innovation, but when they did, the results revolutionized the sport, shaving seconds off previous records.

Clap skates are not the only innovation: pole vaulters have taken advantage of springier, fiberglass poles. To a lesser extent, runners have been helped by better shoes and special elastic tracks that do not absorb as much energy as previous surfaces did. The springy surface returns energy to a runner's stride that would otherwise be consumed by an ordinary track. Still, the improvements possible through these technologies are not as critical as basic athletic ability. Dapena puts the importance of equipment in perspective when he says, "If you ask, 'Would you like to have Michael Johnson's body or his shoes?' I'll take the body."

But materials do make a big difference. Gideon B. Ariel, one of the fathers of biomechanics and the founder of the Olympic Training Center in Colorado Springs, compared the performance of Jesse Owens with that of Carl Lewis. In 1936 Owens ran the 100-meter event in 10.2 seconds, much slower than the 9.86 Lewis achieved in 1991. "Of course, what Jesse Owens was running on was not the same surface that Carl Lewis ran on," Ariel explains. Owens ran on a clay track that absorbed more energy than the modern tracks on which Lewis set his record. "Imagine you're running on the beach in very deep sand. Your joints might be very fast, but you don't make the progress. If you run the same on the road, you will be faster. You're really not faster, you are more efficient—you don't lose as much energy." Ariel was able to analyze films of Owens running and determine that his joints were moving as fast as Lewis's. He determined that had Owens and Lewis run on the same track the results would not have been nearly as lopsided, although Lewis would probably still have run faster.

Pushing the Limits

Given the best training and the best equipment, how fast can a Michael Johnson, Maurice Greene or another genetically gifted athlete hope to run? Ariel addressed this question in 1976. He concentrated on power sports such

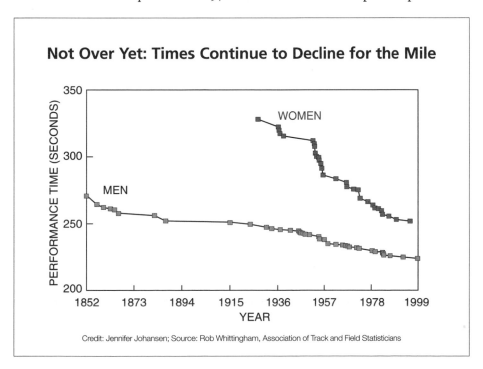

Not Over Yet: Times Continue to Decline for the Mile

Credit: Jennifer Johansen; Source: Rob Whittingham, Association of Track and Field Statisticians

as sprinting and jumping, because, he reasoned, these are most easily analyzed using the tools of Newtonian mechanics. "In the power events, you have anatomical restrictions like the strength of the bones and the strength of the muscles. At some point, at a certain level of force, the human body will not be able to sustain it, and a bone will crack or a tendon will come off," Ariel says. "We use data from various research institutions that show the strength of bones, the strength of connective tissues and stuff like that." To be on the safe side, Ariel decided to increase these estimates by 20 percent and then calculated the breaking point. "It is straightforward mathematics to do this calculation," he says. "I think we are pretty accurate, and the proof is that since 1976 nobody has done better than we predicted, because the human body didn't change." Specifically, Ariel predicted that no one would ever run 100 meters in less than 9.6 seconds, jump higher than 8 feet 5 inches or throw a shot farther than 75 feet 10.25 inches, and so far no person has succeeded in beating those estimates.

The limits in endurance events, which depend more on physiology than mechanics, are far harder to calculate. The reason is that to figure physiological limits requires a deep understanding of metabolism at a cellular level, something that cannot be captured by a video camera. "I'm not sure we are close to the limit," Ariel says. "Somebody might come who will run a sub-four-minute mile for 10 miles, and that would break a world record by an unbelievable amount. If you can do it for one mile, maybe you can build a training routine where you can do it for two, three or four miles."

In the end, most people who have attempted to examine human performance are eventually humbled by the resourcefulness of athletes and the powers of the human body. "Once you study athletics, you learn that it's a vexingly complex issue," says John S. Raglin, a sports psychologist at Indiana

University. "Core performance is not a simple or mundane thing of higher, faster, longer. So many variables enter into the equation, and our understanding in many cases is very, very fundamental. We've got a long way to go." For the foreseeable future, records will still be made to be broken.

Scientific American Presents: Building the Elite Athlete, Fall 2000

The Female Hurt

Women are more vulnerable than men
to certain injuries and may not be getting
proper treatment for them

MARGUERITE HOLLOWAY

"I don't want to hear a bunch of thuds," bellows Deborah Saint-Phard from her corner of the basketball court. Several dozen young women and girls, some barefoot, some in jeans and tank tops, some in full athletic regalia, look sheepish. They jump again, trying to keep their knees slightly bent and facing straight forward, trying to make no noise when their feet hit the floor. "I can hear you landing," Saint-Phard nonetheless admonishes, urging them into a softer touchdown. "Control your jump."

Saint-Phard is a doctor with the Women's Sports Medicine Center at the Hospital for Special Surgery in New York City. She and several colleagues have traveled to this gymnasium in Philadelphia for "Hoop City"—a National Collegiate Athletic Association (NCAA) event—to teach young women how to jump safely. Female athletes, particularly those playing basketball, volleyball and soccer, are between five and eight times more likely than men are to injure their anterior cruciate ligament, or ACL, which stabilizes the knee. Some 20,000 high school girls and 10,000 female college students suffer debilitating knee injuries each year, the majority of which are ACL-related, according to the American Orthopedic Society for Sports Medicine. Tearing the ligament can put an athlete out of the game for months, if not forever.

"This is a huge public health problem for women," says Edward M. Wojtys, an orthopedic surgeon at the University of Michigan. "Fourteen- to 18-year-olds are subjected to injuries that many of them will never recover from, that will affect whether they can walk or exercise at 40 and 50." For this reason, physicians are placing new emphasis on teaching female athletes how to jump in such a way that they strengthen their knees and protect their ACLs. "We have to get them when they are young," Saint-Phard says.

Torn ACLs are just one of the medical problems that plague female athletes. Injuries and ailments that occur with higher incidence in women than in men are garnering more attention as women enter sports in record numbers—not only as Olympians and professionals but for fitness and recreation. Today 135,110 women participate in collegiate athletics, according to the NCAA, up from 29,977 in 1972. The number of girls

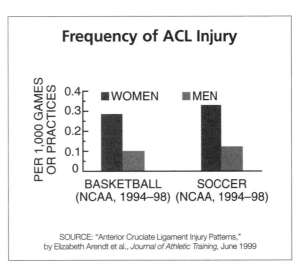

playing high school sports has shot up from 294,015 to 2.5 million in the same time frame. As a result, researchers, physicians and coaches are increasingly recognizing that girls and women engaged in sports have some distinct medical concerns.

This makes perfect sense. Women's bodies are shaped differently than men's, and they are influenced by different hormones. They may be at greater risk not only for ACL tears but for other knee problems, as well as for certain shoulder injuries. Women are also uniquely threatened by a condition called the female athlete triad: disordered eating habits, menstrual dysfunction or the loss of their menstrual cycle, and, as a consequence of these two changes, premature and permanent osteoporosis. "We are seeing 25-year-olds with the bones of 70-year-olds," Saint-Phard says.

Although the passage of Title IX legislation in 1972 required that institutions receiving federal funding devote equal resources to men's and women's sports, it has taken a while for the particular needs of female athletes to emerge. As an example, Wojtys points to the ACL: "It took us 15 to 18 years to realize that this problem existed." Women entering sports even a decade and a half after Title IX received less care from coaches and physicians than male athletes did, says Saint-Phard, who competed in the 1988 Olympic shot-put event. When she was in college, she recalls, "the men's teams got a lot more resources and a different level of coaches than the women's teams."

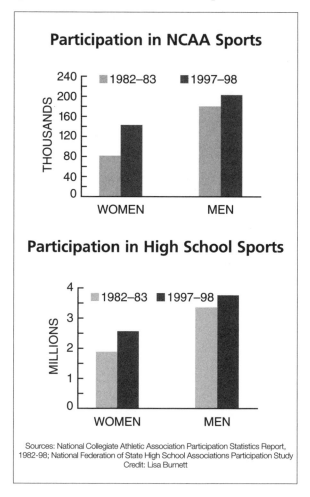

Participation in NCAA Sports

1982–83   1997–98

THOUSANDS

240
200
160
120
80
40
0

WOMEN   MEN

Participation in High School Sports

1982–83   1997–98

MILLIONS

4
3
2
1
0

WOMEN   MEN

Sources: National Collegiate Athletic Association Participation Statistics Report, 1982-98; National Federation of State High School Associations Participation Study
Credit: Lisa Burnett

And today even those conditions that are increasingly well recognized as more problematic for women are not fully understood, and their etiology and treatment remain controversial at times. "There is not enough awareness of the differences," says Regina M. Vidaver of the Society for Women's Health Research. For most of the people treating sports injuries, she explains, "their predominant history is with men."

A spate of studies in the past few years on the ACL and the triad have made clear the need for specialized research and care for women. And the medical field seems to be responding accordingly. The Women's Sports Medicine Center is currently the only one of its kind in the U.S., but it won't be alone for much longer. This year the University of California at Los Angeles will open a center devoted to the medical care of female athletes, and Saint-Phard and her colleagues have had inquiries from universities wanting to start similar programs in Baltimore and Detroit, as well as in Florida, Texas, North Carolina and Tennessee. In addition, this autumn the National Institute of Arthritis and Musculoskeletal and Skin Diseases will solicit research proposals on women and sports—with an emphasis on the long-term consequences of exercise at all levels of participation. This area of medical inquiry is only a beginning, says the institute's Joan A. McGowan. "When you want research in a certain area, you can't just order it up, you have to grow it."

Tearing into ACL Injuries

The most obvious musculoskeletal difference between men and women is the breadth of their hips. Because a woman's pelvis tends to be wider, the muscles that run from the hip down to the knee pull the kneecap (the patella) out to the side more, sometimes causing what is called patellofemoral syndrome—a painful condition that appears to occur more frequently in women. In men, the muscle and bone run more directly vertically, putting less lateral pull on the patella. Some studies also indicate that women's joints and muscles may tend to be more lax than men's; although this adds to greater flexibility, it may mean that female joints and muscles are not necessarily as stable.

Increased laxity and differences in limb alignment may contribute to ACL injuries among female athletes. And yet, even though physicians and coaches first recognized in the 1980s that female athletes were more prone to this injury, there is still no resolution about the cause. "It is an area of controversy," observes Joseph Bosco, an orthopedic surgeon at New York University.

Some experts place the blame squarely on laxity, musculoskeletal configuration and a few other physiological differences. They note that the bony notch the ACL passes through as it attaches to the lower leg bone may be proportionately smaller in women. Other researchers have shown that women typically favor using their quadricep muscles (at the front of the thigh) rather than their hamstrings (at the back of the thigh), an imbalance that may rip the ACL. And still others think the injury is more related to the training women receive, their skill level and their overall fitness. Most, however, agree that it is some combination of several of these factors.

Recent studies indicating that ACL injuries can be prevented by training women to jump differently and to develop their hamstring muscles suggest that inadequate training is at least a large part of the problem. "We train and condition women in the same way that we do the men," says Wojtys, who showed in a 1999 study that women tend not to bend their knees as much as men do when they land a jump, thereby increasing the pressure of the impact on the joints. "They probably need their own training programs."

The Cincinnati Sportsmedicine and Orthopaedic Center focuses on just

The Inside Story on Injury

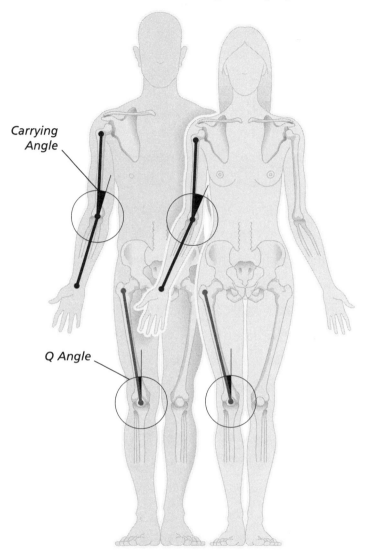

Carrying Angle

Q Angle

The skeletons of women differ from men's most visibly in the width of the pelvis. As a result, women have a wider Q angle (a measure of bone alignment from hip to knee) and carrying angle (from upper to lower arm), which can lead, respectively, to higher rates of knee and elbow or shoulder injuries.

Credit: Samuel Velasco

such an approach. In 1996 Frank R. Noyes and his colleagues there followed 11 high school girl volleyball players who went through Sportsmetrics, a grueling six-week jump-training program the researchers had created. They found that all the participants improved their hamstring strength and that all but one were able to reduce their landing forces, placing less stress on their knees as a result (and achieving the "quiet landing" Saint-Phard was looking for in Philadelphia).

The investigators went on to follow two new groups of female athletes—those who did this strength training and those who did not—as well as a group of male athletes without Sportsmetrics. In an article published last year in the *American Journal of Sports Medicine*, the authors, led by Timothy E. Hewett, reported that only two of the 366 trained female athletes (and two of the 434 male athletes) suffered serious knee injuries, whereas 10 of the 463 untrained women did. They concluded that specially trained female athletes were 1.3 to 2.4 times more likely to have a serious knee injury than the male athletes were, whereas the untrained females were 4.8 to 5.8 times more likely.

The idea that better, or perhaps more, training could have a strong effect on injury rates is supported by work with another set of women: army recruits. According to a recent study by Nicole S. Bell of the Boston University School of Public Health, female recruits were twice as likely to suffer injuries during basic combat training than men were—and two and a half times more likely to have serious injuries. The injuries were not only knee-related but included sprains and stress fractures of the foot and lower leg. Bell found that, overall, the women were not in as good shape as the men were and that a lack of fitness was associated with injury rates in both sexes. Many girls don't participate in sports as they are growing up, typically getting started only in late junior high school or beyond, Noyes says. "The boys have been running around playing tanks and guns, and the girls have been playing house," he says. "That goes along with the theory that girls are less fit."

Despite the growing consensus about the benefits of jump training, the approach is in limited use. Saint-Phard and her colleagues have led the injury prevention workshop they held in Philadelphia in schools around New York City. But they reach a very small group of young women and coaches. The challenge, Noyes and others note, is getting to the wider community of coaches, parents and trainers. "We need training programs nationwide," Noyes insists. He says that although some coaches are happy to see him, the rest consider knee-strength training a six-week regimen that just holds up team practice.

Noyes is also working to redress another sports medicine imbalance. Historically, men have been more likely than women to have knee surgery. Noyes believes that there are two reasons. First, knee surgery used to be a difficult procedure with often poor outcomes, so it was limited to athletes who really "needed" it—in other words, professional male athletes. Second, there has been a perception among physicians that women would not fare as well during the often painful surgery and recovery. So Noyes and his colleagues decided to examine the responses of both men and women to ACL surgery. They determined that although women took slightly longer to heal, both sexes fared equally well in the long run.

Noyes's work on surgery outcomes and the growing consensus about the importance of neuromuscular control appear to have shifted some attention away from another area of ACL injury investigation: hormonal influences. Researchers have found that the ACL has estrogen and progesterone receptors—target sites that respond to those two hormones. In studies in animals and in vitro, they have discovered that the presence of estrogen decreases the synthesis of collagen fibers, the building blocks of ligaments. It also increases the levels of another hormone, relaxin, which in turn adds to the disorganization of collagen fibers. This change in the ligaments makes the ACL more flexible and, according to the hypothesis, more vulnerable to injury.

This view seems supported by some studies, including one by Wojtys published two years ago in the *American Journal of Sports Medicine*. He and his team questioned 40 women with ACL injuries; the majority of the tears occurred during ovulation, when estrogen levels were highest. Other studies show some increased muscle laxity in ovulating women, but nothing dramatic.

Wojtys's study has been contested as suspect because it was based on such a small sample size, because the women's ages were so variable and because the researchers were relying on the athletes' recollections. And Wojtys himself agrees that nothing is definite. "It is not something you can hang your hat on," he says, noting, however, that other studies indicate that women on birth-control pills have a much lower rate of injury—presumably because they don't ovulate and their estrogen levels are lower. "It is indirect evidence; none of it is confirmatory. But to ignore it and not investigate doesn't make any sense," he says. Wojtys, whose interest in women's sports medicine was catalyzed by his two daughters' love of sports, says that he is not averse to being proved wrong and adds that, in fact, he hopes he is.

"Estrogen probably has some role," notes Jo A. Hannafin, orthopedic director at the Women's Sports Medicine Center. But, she says, no one is applying the studies' findings to the court—limiting, say, what time of month a player should or should not play. The hormonal result "just reinforces old stereotypes," Bosco adds. "It takes weeks and weeks for the effects [of estrogen] to be seen, so it doesn't make sense. We still strongly encourage women to participate in athletics over the whole month."

Treating the Triad

Estrogen's role in the other major health threat to female athletes is not at all controversial. Exercise or poor eating, or both, can cause an athlete's body to develop an energy deficit, become stressed and lose essential nutrients. Any or all of these changes can cause levels of follicular-stimulating and luteinizing hormones to fall and ovulation to therefore cease. Absent their menstrual cycles, young athletes do not have the requisite estrogen at precisely the time they need the hormone the most to help retain calcium and lay down bone. By the age of 17, nearly all a young woman's bone has been established, explains Melinda M. Manore, a professor of nutrition at Arizona State University. If an athlete's level of estrogen remains low, she can start to lose bone mass at a rapid rate, which can lead to stress fractures and, if the process is not curbed, premature osteoporosis.

The phrase "female athlete triad" was coined in 1992 by participants at an American College of Sports Medicine meeting. Since then, anecdotal reports have indicated that the occurrence of the triad is on the rise. "I think young women are more and more aware of their body size," Manore says. Furthermore, female athletes are especially vulnerable. Eating disorders—such as obsessive dieting, calorie restriction or aversion to fat (all labeled disordered eating), as well as anorexia and bulimia (the so-called classic eating disorders)—are disproportionately high in girls and women who participate regularly in sports.

Averaged across various sports, some 30 percent of these individuals have an eating problem, as opposed to 10 to 15 percent of the general population—although no one knows for sure, because no large-scale studies on prevalence have been conducted in the U.S. The proportion may be as high as 70 percent in some sports. "High achievers, perfectionists, goal setters, people who are compulsive and determined—those are the things that characterize our best athletes," says Margot Putukian, a team physician at Pennsylvania State University. Those are also the very qualities that often lead people into problem eating.

And athletic culture—particularly for swimmers, runners, skiers, rowers and gymnasts—only continues to reinforce these behaviors and expectations. Many coaches encourage their athletes to lose weight so they can be faster or have less mass to move through acrobatic maneuvers. According to a recent study, female gymnasts weigh 20 pounds less than those in the 1970s did. And many female athletes at all levels see losing their period as a badge of honor. "They don't see it as a negative," Putukian explains. "They see it as something that happens when you get in shape, a sign that you are training adequately." What they also don't see is what is happening to their bones—until they develop stress fractures. "They fly through their adolescent years with no knowledge of why being too thin is dangerous," Saint-Phard says.

Treating the triad is challenging, and, as Putukian notes, "there is not a lot of great data to tell us what is the best thing." Researchers now recognize that female athletes experiencing these problems need the combined talents of a physician, a nutritionist and, if they have bulimia or anorexia, a psychologist—a multidisciplinary team that most schools and colleges lack. "When you have a kid who has an eating disorder, it is very frustrating," Putukian says. "It is reversible if you catch it early on, irreversible if you don't." She tells her athletes—who are all questioned about their menses and their eating habits during their initial physical—that if they haven't had their period for three months, they are in danger. Putukian tries to get them on a birth-control pill and works with them to change their eating habits if they have a problem. But although the pill restores some hormonal activity, it does not provide the requisite levels for normal bone development. And hormone replacement therapy, which is used by some physicians, has not been extensively tested in young women.

Nevertheless, Putukian notes that athletes may be easier to treat than women in the general population because there is an incentive: competition. "It is an incredible tool," she says. "You can help kids come back." Putukian has refused to let several athletes compete until they got their weight up to healthy levels; their desire to participate drove them to improve their eating habits.

Putukian, Manore and others would like to see young women better educated about the consequences of excessive dieting and amenorrhea. They admit that little can be done about the cultural pressures facing young women—the unrealistic icons of emaciated beauty that destroy many self-images. But they believe that if girls understand that they may be jeopardizing their freedom to take a simple jog in their 30s without fracturing their osteoporotic hips or leg bones, they will change their behavior. The investigators hope that athletes will focus on how they feel and how they perform, rather than on how much they weigh. But as with the jump-training program to prevent ACL injuries, there remains a great divide between the medical community's recommendations and the reality of the track or court or gymnasium. Only when those are fully integrated will Title IX have truly fulfilled its promise.

Scientific American Presents: Building the Elite Athlete, Fall 2000

The Mystery of Muscle

GLENN ZORPETTE

A little over two decades ago a grinning, oiled Arnold Schwarzenegger, with the motion picture *Pumping Iron*, hauled bodybuilding out of the dingy gyms and into the mainstream of U.S. popular culture. During more or less the same period, anabolic steroids started infiltrating bodybuilding, turning musclemen into big-jawed, moon-faced freaks, and strength-training machines began making weight training safer and more appealing to the masses.

The U.S. has not been the same since. Strength training has persisted as few movements have in recent U.S. history, reshaping popular views of physical beauty and male feelings of self-esteem. In 1994 an article in *Psychology Today* declared that "there seems to be emerging a single standard of beauty for men today: a hypermasculine, muscled, powerfully shaped body." Since then, the trend has only intensified.

In 1995 weight training replaced riding a stationary bicycle as the most popular kind of exercise among American adults. The same year the number of males in the U.S. who worked out with weights at least 100 days a year reached 11.6 million, up from 7.4 million in 1987, according to American Sports Data in Hartsdale, N.Y. And more recently, the market for dietary supplements aimed at weight lifters and bodybuilders has grown explosively, led by a chalky powder called creatine monohydrate [*see* "Sports Supplements: Bigger Muscles without the Acne," on page 33].

Although the number of women who regularly use weights has roughly tripled in the past decade, the superior ability of men to add muscle to their bodies has ensured that weight training remains inextricably linked to the male image and feelings of self-worth. And in recent years, several disturbing aspects of this link have become clear. Use of anabolic steroids is up, as are cases of muscle dysmorphia, a puzzling disorder in which abundantly muscled people see themselves as scrawny and become increasingly obsessed with weight training [*see* "You See Brawny, I See Scrawny," on page 35].

Along with the cultural appreciation of muscle has come a surge of work aimed at understanding the biology of muscles. The vast majority of researchers in this area are studying anatomical or physiological aspects of exercise related to aging, the effects of diet, dietary supplements and so on. A large group is also studying heart muscle tissue, a subject that bears strongly on cardiac diseases. Oddly enough, what might seem to be the most compelling issue in muscle science in this physique-obsessed era—the biochemistry of bulking up—has but a tiny band of full-time devotees.

Nevertheless, their research has yielded some impressive and even startling results of late. For example, researchers at the Royal Free and University College Medical School of University College London recently cloned a kind of hormone, which they call mechano-growth factor, that appears to be a significant link in the still largely mysterious ways in which muscle cells respond biochemically to mechanical stress by becoming stronger and thicker.

The University College researchers themselves view their discovery with a mixture of enthusiasm and uneasiness. On the one hand, the findings could be invaluable for treating muscular dystrophy and possibly age-related muscle loss. At the same time, the discovery seems likely to usher in a new age in performance-enhancing drugs, one that sports officials have anticipated with dread.

Stimulating the production of mechano-growth factor in specific muscles would increase their mass. Doing so would require only the injection of bits of human DNA into the muscles. Because the muscle cells would have already contained the DNA naturally, sports officials would find it difficult, if not impossible, to detect the injections. Thus, the development promises to create the ultimate muscle-building drug—one that, like anabolic steroids, could build muscles even without strenuous exercise.

"We've cloned the magic substance that makes muscles grow," says Geoffrey Goldspink, the leader of the University College group that identified and reproduced the growth factor. In the not too distant future, he adds, "American footballers and athletes in all countries will probably be using this method. It will be abused, I'm sure. It is a great worry to me."

How Muscles Contract

The recent findings at University College and elsewhere on skeletal muscle are the latest in a chain of discoveries stretching back at least to the 1950s. Researchers have laid out a detailed if incomplete understanding of skeletal muscle: what it is, how it works, how it grows and develops, and—most intriguingly—how it alters itself in response to exercise.

Although it is only one of three categories of muscle in the human body, skeletal muscle is what most people think of as "muscle." The other two kinds are cardiac muscle, which powers the heart, and smooth muscle, which lines the arteries and parts of the stomach, intestine, uterus and other bodily components (its relatively slow, sustained contractions move food through the digestive system, for example).

Groups of skeletal muscles contracting against a scaffold of bone, all coordinated by the nervous system, do the work of lifting, playing the piano, moving an eyeball or throwing a right cross. Muscle is the most abundant tissue in the body, a distinction that makes it the body's largest store of a variety of key substances, such as amino acids, which are the building blocks of protein. For this reason, among others, the consequences of muscle loss in the elderly go beyond frailty to include such problems as weakened immune systems.

Skeletal muscle cells, also known as muscle fibers, are rather unusual in many respects, not least of which is that they have multiple nuclei. They are also comparatively huge, at approximately 50 microns in diameter and up to tens of centimeters long. Most of the cells' cytoplasm (the gelatinous part outside the nucleus but within the membrane) consists of elements called myofibrils [see illustration on pages 26–27]. Organized by the hundreds or thousands inside the muscle fiber, myofibrils are often about the same length as the muscle cells but only one to two microns in diameter.

Myofibrils are the contractile elements of muscle. In other words, a muscle contracts—and does work—when the lengths of all its myofibrils shrink forcefully in response to nerve impulses. To understand how the myofibrils do this requires an understanding of yet smaller elements within the myofibrils. These components, called sarcomeres, are the contractile units of muscle; a myofibril contracts when all its sarcomeres do so. Sarcomeres are about 2.2 microns long and are linked end to end to make up a myofibril.

Like Russian nesting dolls, muscle's components keep getting smaller: within each sarcomere are two protein molecules, known as myosin and actin. It is the interaction of these two molecules, primarily, that makes a sarcomere contract.

Myosin, the most abundant protein in muscle, is shaped like a tadpole, with a large head and a long, thin tail. Many of these proteins make up what is known as a myosin thick filament, the central component of a sarcomere. In a thick filament the many myosin proteins are arranged with their tails

Sarcomere's key components are myosin and actin. These protein molecules slide over one another, telescopically, as the sarcomere contracts (top) and uncontracts (bottom). The myosin heads, which protrude outward from the filament's central stem, lock onto sites on the closest actin filament. The heads release one site and grip the next, "walking" the actin molecule over the myosin.

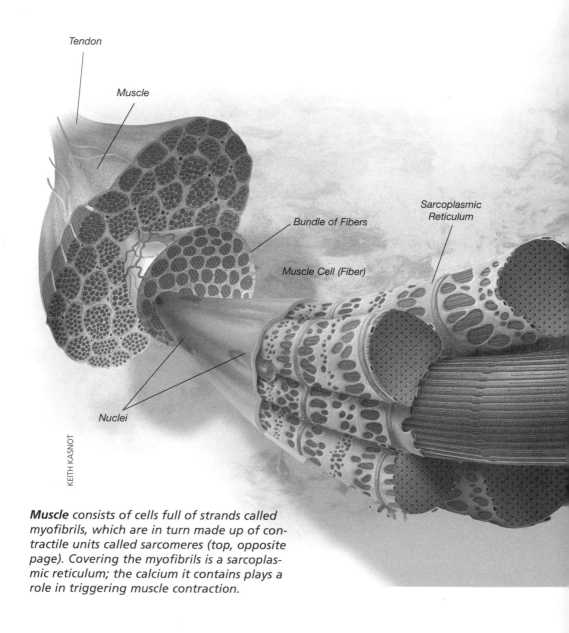

Tendon

Muscle

Bundle of Fibers

Sarcoplasmic Reticulum

Muscle Cell (Fiber)

Nuclei

KEITH KASNOT

Muscle consists of cells full of strands called myofibrils, which are in turn made up of contractile units called sarcomeres (top, opposite page). Covering the myofibrils is a sarcoplasmic reticulum; the calcium it contains plays a role in triggering muscle contraction.

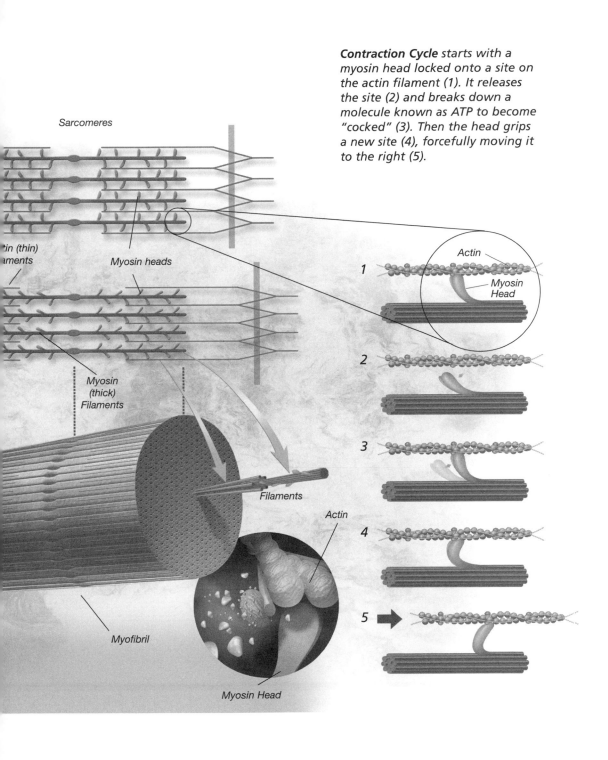

Sarcomeres

Contraction Cycle *starts with a myosin head locked onto a site on the actin filament (1). It releases the site (2) and breaks down a molecule known as ATP to become "cocked" (3). Then the head grips a new site (4), forcefully moving it to the right (5).*

*tin (thin)
aments

Myosin heads

Actin

Myosin
Head

1

Myosin
(thick)
Filaments

2

3

Filaments

Actin

4

5

Myofibril

Myosin Head

bundled together, like a bunch of pencils held in a fist and with the heads sticking out to the side.

In the sarcomere the ends of the thick filament are surrounded by molecules of actin, also elongated and helical, and parallel to the myosin [*see* illustration on pages 26–27]. During muscle contraction, a sarcomere shortens like a collapsing telescope as the actin filaments at each end of the myosin thick filament slide toward the thick filament's center.

The motive force that pulls the actins inward is exerted by the myosin heads. Each myosin head locks onto specific sites on the actin molecule. The head "walks" the actin molecule over the bundles of myosin tails, step by step, by relinquishing its grip on one site on the actin and grabbing and pulling the adjacent site [see illustration, page 27 at right]. In effect, the myosin heads are like so many oars that, marvelously synchronized, paddle the actin filaments to move them.

The fuel for this molecular motor is adenosine triphosphate (ATP). In a contracting sarcomere, an ATP molecule combines with a myosin head and breaks down into adenosine diphosphate (ADP) and a phosphate ion. From this reaction comes the energy necessary to release the myosin head from the actin molecule, to move the head to the next binding site and to help pull the actin molecule that distance. The ratchetlike cycle can happen five times a second in a rapidly contracting muscle. As the cycles occur, various reactions convert the ADP back to ATP to keep fueling the contraction.

Three Kinds of Skeletal Muscle

Healthy adults have at least three main types of skeletal muscle cells, which differ primarily in the kind of myosin at the core of their sarcomeres. These three cell types, like the myosin variants they contain, are designated I, IIa and IIx (also known as IId).

Type I muscle cells are also known as slow fibers, because their kind of myosin converts ATP to ADP relatively slowly and derives energy from the reaction efficiently. Muscles that must contract repeatedly for long periods, such as those of the back and legs, are rich in type I fibers. For example, the soleus, which extends from the central calf area to the ankle, is almost entirely type I. It comes into play not only for walking and running but even for simply standing.

Type I muscle cells, which are critical for any kind of aerobic exertion, have large numbers of mitochondria, specialized cellular functionaries that use nutrients and oxygen to convert ADP back into ATP. Type I muscle fibers are therefore the narrowest, because their constant need to feed the mitochondria with nutrients and oxygen and to remove their waste limits how wide the fiber can be. These fibers also have a great deal of myoglobin, a protein that acts as a short-term store of oxygen for the cells. (The leg and thigh meat of a chicken, rich in type I muscle, gets its dark coloration from the myoglobin.)

The other two myosin varieties are "fast." They predominate in muscles, such as those of the biceps, capable of more powerful but less frequent contractions. One of the key necessities for sustaining high-power output even briefly is a method of rapidly replenishing ATP, the cells' energy source. Type II fibers have variable amounts of mitochondria, but they also exploit a much faster process, called glycolysis, to provide the energy the muscle needs. Basically, glycolysis releases energy for making ATP by breaking down sugars only partially but without need for oxygen.

The type II fibers differ mainly in their oxidative properties. Type IIa fibers have more mitochondria and are thus more similar to type I. Because of the extra mitochondria, type IIa can sustain an output of power longer than can the type IIx fibers, which are "faster," more powerful and more quickly fatigued.

The bodily distribution of the different muscle fiber types is not fixed. It depends on the body's regular activities, and it changes if they do. This ability of the body to alter itself is an important part of its complex, genetically based response to mechanical stressors and signals. Take an extreme example: a fitness enthusiast who gives up doing squat thrusts and begins training to run a marathon. According to Brenda Russell of the University of Illinois at Chicago, who did pioneering investigation in this area in the early 1980s, the runner would gradually replace much of the fast, type IIx fibers in his quadriceps and calves with the slower, more oxidative type IIa fiber. The change would occur because the nuclei of the muscle cells in his legs would stop specifying production of type IIx myosin and start prompting for the type IIa myosin. In more technical terms, the nuclei would stop "expressing" the gene that through a chain of events triggers the cell to assemble amino acids into the type IIx myosin. Instead the nuclei would express the gene that specifies the IIa type.

Bulking Up

Researchers know relatively little about how the body translates mechanical stresses into increased muscle mass. Recent findings, however, have shed light on parts of the process while generating some intriguing theories and a few controversies.

One of those areas of contention is whether the number of muscle cells in a body is fixed for life. Although a small group of researchers disagrees, the widely accepted view is that the number of muscle cells cannot increase significantly, because the cells cannot split apart to form completely new fibers.

(Their multiple nuclei may make the process infeasible.) Because a muscle cannot produce more fibers, the only way it can grow in response to exercise is for the individual fibers to become thicker. This thickening can be thought of as the body defending itself against a mechanical stress by enlarging the structural members so that they can generate more contractile force.

With continued weight training, the type II muscle fibers grow ever thicker by adding more myofibrils. This thickening initially involves the longitudinal splitting of myofibrils into two daughter myofibrils, a process that occurs over and over if the mechanical stresses continue. Enormous amounts of myosin, actin and myriad other proteins are needed to create entirely new myofibrils. But the amount of protein, and therefore the number of myofibrils, that the existing muscle cell nuclei can help create and maintain is limited.

In cardiac muscle, that limit is absolute. In skeletal muscle, it is not. Scattered among the many nuclei on the surface of a skeletal muscle fiber are so-called satellite cells. They are largely separate from the muscle cell and, unlike it, have only the usual one nucleus apiece. Thus, they can replicate by dividing. In the mid-1970s Véra Hanzliková and her colleagues at the Czechoslovak Academy of Sciences in Prague discovered that these satellite cells proliferate in response to the stresses of muscle growth.

As they multiply, some of these cells remain as satellites on the fiber, but others, incredibly, become incorporated into it. Their nuclei become indistinguishable from the muscle cell's other nuclei. With these additional nuclei, the fiber is able to churn out more proteins and create more myofibrils. Most researchers now believe that this recruitment of satellite cells is a significant factor in the muscle growth that comes from weight lifting.

Satellite cells figure in another controversy: whether damage to muscles is necessary for enlargement (a phenomenon known as hypertrophy). A popular theory contends that it is: according to this view, rigorous exercise inflicts tiny "microtears" in muscle fibers. Calcium ions enter the ripped area, initiating biochemical cascades that break down the existing proteins to leave a less ragged gap. The tiny opening, meanwhile, releases a specific protein—the very same one that Goldspink has dubbed mechano-growth factor but that others have called hepatocyte growth factor or scatter factor. In the mid-1990s Richard Bischoff of Washington University found that at least in cultured cells, this growth factor attracts satellite cells to its source, which in muscle would be the damaged area.

Some of these satellite cells incorporate themselves into the muscle tissue and begin producing proteins to fill the gap. Significantly, the number of nuclei passing from the satellite cells into the damaged area of the fiber is greater than the number of nuclei lost when the gap opened up. As a result, in that part of the fiber, more protein can be produced and supported. Gradually, as more microtears are repaired, the overall number of nuclei grows—as does the fiber itself.

Muscle-making Machinery

This "damage" model of muscle cell growth is by no means the only one that can explain hypertrophy; it is at best only one of many, perhaps dozens, of processes at work in exercise-induced muscle growth. For example, a fair amount of speculation, and at least a modest amount of research, focuses on the mechanical connections between muscle cells and surrounding tissue. These connectors are the tendons and the focal adhesion complex, a series of some 30 proteins that connects the cell's skeleton (the "cytoskeleton") with its exterior supportive "scaffolding," the extra-cellular matrix.

Sports Supplements:
Bigger Muscles without the Acne

Steroid alternatives have become an $800-million market

W eight lifting used to be pretty simple. You went to a dingy, seedy room on the other side of the railroad tracks, you put on ragged cotton clothes, and you hoisted, heaved and herniated to your heart's content. Of course, in those days, Burt Lancaster and Jack LaLanne were paragons of physical masculinity.

Today better understanding of nutrition and muscular development has complicated life for weight lifters. Most notably, it has given rise to so-called sports supplements, a category comprising hundreds of different pills, powders and the odd potion that supposedly enhance physical performance. Last year Americans spent some $800 million on sports supplements, not including sports nutrition bars and electrolyte replacement drinks, according to Grant Ferrier, editor of the *Nutrition Business Journal* in San Diego.

Sports supplements aimed at weight lifters are doing particularly well, thanks in part to clinical trials that have proved that at least a few of the supplements actually do help increase strength and muscle mass or promote the repair of muscle tissue.

"Supplements are a tool for making an exercise program work," says Bill Phillips, the relentlessly motivational 34-year-old CEO of Experimental and Applied Sciences, the largest marketer of sports supplements. "And when an exercise program works, it is one of the most empowering things an adult can experience."

At best, supplements provide the elevated energy levels and possibly the tissue-repairing help that lets weight lifters lift a little more weight, do a few more repetitions or train a little more often. The muscle-mass gains possible are not on a par with those of anabolic steroids. But supplements have the advantages of being legal, much less expensive and a lot less harmful.

No two weight lifters seem to have the same supplement regimen. But the one thing almost all of them have in common is creatine, which accounted for $180 million of the $800 million spent on all sports supplements in 1998, according to Ferrier. Most weight lifters are also consuming some kind of protein supplement, such as whey powder or ordinary sports nutrition bars.

Creatine occurs naturally in the body. It plays a role in muscle contraction, which is energized by a molecule called adenosine triphosphate (ATP). When ATP breaks down, giving up one of its three phosphates, it releases the energy used by the muscle cell to contract. The small amount of ATP stored in a muscle is used up instantaneously during strenuous exertion. Fortunately, muscles contain creatine phosphate, which donates its phosphate and the necessary energy to replenish the ATP.

Eventually you tire out when, among other things, your supply of creatine phosphate dwindles. But by taking creatine supplements, weight lifters and sprinters can at least marginally increase the amount of creatine phosphate in their muscles, enabling them to exert themselves a little harder. Although no one has been able to prove that creatine has any harmful side effects, no study has lasted more than a few years.

The biggest seller in the prohormone category is 4-androstenedione, which became one of the longest and strangest household words in history after Mark McGwire's admission that he was using it. The substance is just one of a growing family of over-the-counter steroids; other products in this category include 5-androstenedione, 4-androstenediol, 5-androstenediol, 19-4-norandrostenedione and 19-5-norandrostenediol. Yet another product, DHEA (dehydroepiandrosterone), like 4-androstenedione, is often used by people seeking to boost their sex drive.

The main difference between these prohormones and traditional anabolic steroids is that the prohormones are converted in the liver and testes to testosterone, the body's key hormone for muscle building. Anabolic steroids, in contrast, are nothing more than synthetic versions of testosterone. Because of this hormonal action, prohormones can have mildly steroidal side effects, such as acne, a swollen prostate and hair growth in unusual places. Some evidence suggests that prohormones temporarily elevate testosterone levels, at least marginally, but no one knows if these higher levels translate into greater muscle mass.

You See Brawny, I See Scrawny

Big bruisers with a self-image problem

The ascendance of muscle as a key ingredient of male allure has had ramifications both good and bad. Take the countless aging squires and he-men who've turned to weight training mainly out of vanity: they have unwittingly improved their metabolic rates, bone strength, connective tissue and other important bodily components. At the same time, though, a distressing self-image disorder—which afflicts men disproportionately—has become pervasive enough of late to be the subject of dozens of articles in the academic and general-interest press.

At first description, the malady seems almost comical: imagine a 250-pound bruiser with rippling, rocky muscles and a body-fat percentage hovering around 7.5. Now imagine that the guy thinks he is so scrawny that he only wears loose-fitting clothes to cover up what he sees as a shamefully skinny body. But muscle dysmorphia, as the condition is known, is not very funny. Like anorexia nervosa, the disproportionately feminine disorder to which it is often compared, muscle dysmorphia can lead to complete social withdrawal and, in the most extreme cases, to suicide.

Muscle dysmorphia and anorexia are both part of a larger group of disorders in which the afflicted fixate despairingly on a facial feature, body part or their entire bodies. Harrison G. Pope, Jr., the psychiatrist who has done more than anyone else to uncover and describe the condition, says you can spot muscle dysmorphics by their "pathological preoccupation with their degree of muscularity." Pope, who is probably the only Harvard Medical School professor who can squat 400 pounds, pumps iron six days a week. He himself does not have muscle dysmorphia, he says. (But he did ask *Scientific American Presents* not to disclose his height, weight and body-fat percentage.)

In his studies with volunteers recruited from Boston-area weight rooms, Pope has encountered people "who had not dined in a restaurant in years, because they could not tolerate eating something for which they did not know the precise protein, fat and carbohydrate content." Although use of anabolic steroids is not at all universal among muscle dysmorphics, Pope found "many who would persist in taking anabolic steroids or drugs for fat loss even if they were getting pronounced side effects." Such as? Well, high cholesterol, hard arteries and teeny testicles in men, and beards and rich baritone voices in women.

The anecdotes go on. Pope and his colleagues have encountered dysmorphics who left high-powered jobs in law or business because their careers were taking away too much time from the gym. They've come across muscle dysmorphics in the 230- to 290-pound range who were so ashamed of their puniness that they hardly ever left their homes, preferring instead to adhere to an indoor regimen of weight lifting in the basement interrupted mainly for periodic protein consumption. The underground nature of the condition makes it virtually impossible to estimate how many people have it, Pope says.

How do you distinguish muscle dysmorphia from good old hormone-fueled enthusiasm? One of Pope's experiences suggests a method. To recruit volunteers for a study a couple years back, he put up handbills in Boston-area weight rooms seeking out people who could bench press their own weight 10 times. Hardly any of the respondents had dysmorphia. He then repeated the procedure, again asking for people who could bench their own weight 10 times—but who also thought they were "small." This time, almost all the 24 respondents were dysmorphic.

Mechanical stresses on the tendons and focal adhesion complex are believed to initiate intricate processes that affect the protein-making machinery of muscle cells. Understanding these theories requires some background on the machinery.

One of the key steps in the creation of a protein is transcription. It occurs in a cell's nucleus when a gene's information (encoded in DNA, the "blueprint" for protein production) is copied as a kind of molecule called messenger RNA (mRNA). The mRNA then carries this information outside the nucleus to structures called ribosomes, which assemble amino acids into the protein—myosin or actin, say—specified by that gene. This latter process is called translation.

But what triggers transcription? For muscle and many other tissues, the answer is an array of extraordinarily complex biochemical pathways involving a dizzying number of proteins. Some of the key proteins are sex hormones, such as testosterone, thyroid hormones, insulinlike growth factors, fibroblast growth factor and transcription factors. Some of these proteins are produced in organs such as the liver and circulate throughout the body; others are created locally, in specific muscle tissue, in response to exercise or stretching of that tissue.

These hormones, growth factors and transcription factors act in a variety of ways, often in conjunction with one another, to promote protein production. For example, sex hormones appear to work with particular transcription factors to turn on certain genes. These transcription factors are generally in the cytoplasm or in the nucleus itself. Their combination with a testosterone molecule enables them to bind to locations on the chromosome, called promoter regions, that "turn on" a nearby gene and trigger transcription. Because anabolic steroids are merely synthetic versions of testosterone, this pathway is the one they initiate and exploit to build muscle.

Other factors work by doubling up. In 1995 Frank W. Booth and James Carson of the University of Texas–Houston Health Science Center found that when two identical molecules of serum response factor combine in a muscle cell, they form a kind of biochemical "key." The keyhole in this case is a gene in the nucleus. When the double molecule attaches itself, the gene becomes active and begins producing more mRNA for a certain protein. In this case, the protein is actin. "It's a pretty novel finding," Booth says. "It's only the seventh transcription factor described in hypertrophy."

Other pathways are more complex. Some crucial ones begin with the binding of growth factors to receptors. Receptors are specialized proteins that poke through a cell's membrane. When the part outside the cell binds with a specific molecule, it activates a series of chemical reactions inside the cell. For example, the binding of a growth factor to a receptor activates cascades of enzymes, called kinases, that modify other proteins in the cytoplasm that in turn bind to promoter regions on the chromosome and otherwise regulate the expression of genes.

One of the most important growth factors is insulinlike growth factor-1 (IGF-1). During the first few years of life, IGF-1 produced by the liver circulates throughout the body, rapidly expanding essentially all its muscle fibers. The amount of this circulating, liver-produced IGF-1 eventually declines sharply, ending the early-life spurt. For hypertrophy, the free ride is then over, and only exercise can add (and, eventually, merely maintain) muscle mass. According to University College's Goldspink, IGF-1 and other growth factors continue to play a major role, but they are released only locally in muscle during exercise. For example, IGF-1 concentrations are high around muscle-fiber microtears caused by exercise.

According to Goldspink, mechano-growth factor is one of the most important of these locally acting factors. The University College researchers cloned the gene that leads to the production of mechano-growth factor, using a standard biological technique to insert the gene into muscle cells. The gene for mechano-growth factor was incorporated into a plasmid, a circular piece of DNA, which acted like a teeny Trojan horse. Injected into a mouse's leg, the engineered gene infiltrated muscle cells and induced them to produce more of the growth factor. Within two weeks, the muscle mass in the mouse's leg increased by 15 percent—without exercise.

Goldspink's interest is in treating degenerative diseases such as muscular dystrophy. But he notes ruefully of his accomplishment: "This will be the way they reshape athletes in the future."

Mechanical-Chemical Link

Researchers know very little about the mechanical-chemical link that translates stress on muscle fibers into locally higher levels of mechano-growth factor and countless other biochemicals. But earlier this year Booth and Martin Flück, now at the University of Bern in Switzerland, made a significant discovery. The finding involved focal adhesion kinase, one of the 30 proteins in the focal adhesion complex that connects the structural elements inside cells with the matrix outside them. In muscle cells undergoing hypertrophy, the researchers learned, the amount of this enzyme doubled. "It could be the mechanical-chemical link," Booth speculates, "because the stress on the kinases could release signaling factors, which could go to the nucleus to trigger the production of more messenger RNA" and therefore more protein.

Perhaps more important, the kinase could also trigger a cascade of biochemical reactions that ultimately signal ribosomes directly to produce proteins. These proteins would be the product of translation alone, without any immediately prior gene activity in the nucleus. "We think, and a lot of others think, that the initial response when a muscle is loaded is to increase translation," Booth says. He adds that this more efficient process would, instead of transcribing new mRNA "templates" from the genes, simply reuse existing mRNA already in the cytoplasm to direct protein production.

Although their numbers are small, researchers studying the cellular and molecular biology of skeletal muscle are making important gains as they attempt to unravel the complex mystery of muscle. Over the next decade or so, their work will produce a more complete picture of how one of the most basic of human systems grows, develops and alters itself in response to changing stimuli. In addition to intellectual satisfaction, there will almost certainly be treatments, if not cures, for a host of degenerative diseases.

And if the history of anabolic steroids is a guide, there will also be a new kind of drug abuse problem—one that will be exceedingly difficult to monitor. Science will soon bring high-stakes athletics to a troubling threshold, beyond which the ground rules of competition could be forever altered.

Scientific American Presents Men: The Scientific Truth, Summer 1999

Muscle, Genes and Athletic Performance

*The cellular biology of muscle helps to explain
why a particular athlete wins and suggests what future
athletes might do to better their odds*

JESPER L. ANDERSEN, PETER SCHJERLING AND BENGT SALTIN

"On your marks!" A hush falls as 60,000 pairs of eyes are fixed on eight of the fastest men on earth. The date is August 22, 1999, and the runners are crouched at the starting line of the 100-meter final at the track-and-field world championships in Seville, Spain.

"Get set!" The crack of the gun echoes in the warm evening air, and the crowd roars as the competitors leap from their blocks. Just 9.80 seconds later the winner streaks past the finish line. On this particular day, it is Maurice Greene, a 25-year-old athlete from Los Angeles.

Why, we might ask, is Maurice Greene, and not Bruny Surin of Canada, who finished second, the fastest man on earth? After all, both men have trained incessantly for this moment for years, maintaining an ascetic regimen based on exercise, rest, a strict diet and little else. The answer, of course, is a complex one, touching on myriad small details such as the athletes' mental outlook on race day and even the design of their running shoes. But in a sprint, dependent as it is on raw power, one of the biggest single contributors to victory is physiological: the muscle fibers in Greene's legs, particularly his thighs, are able to generate slightly more power for the brief duration of the sprint than can those of his competitors.

Recent findings in our laboratories and elsewhere have expanded our knowledge of how human muscle adapts to exercise or the lack of it and the extent to which an individual's muscle can alter itself to meet different challenges—such as the long struggle of a marathon or the explosive burst of a sprint. The information helps us understand why an athlete like Greene triumphs and also gives us insights into the range of capabilities of ordinary people. It even sheds light on the perennial issue of whether elite runners, swimmers, cyclists and cross-country skiers are born different from the rest of us or whether proper training and determination could turn almost anyone into a champion.

Skeletal muscle is the most abundant tissue in the human body and also one of the most adaptable. Vigorous training with weights can double or triple a muscle's size, whereas disuse, as in space travel, can shrink it by 20 percent in two weeks. The many biomechanical and biochemical phenomena behind these adaptations are enormously complex, but decades of research have built up a reasonably complete picture of how muscles respond to athletic training.

What most people think of as a muscle is actually a bundle of cells, also known as fibers, kept together by collagen tissue. A single fiber of skeletal muscle consists of a membrane, many scattered nuclei that contain the genes and lie just under the membrane along the length of the fiber, and thousands of inner strands called myofibrils that constitute the cytoplasm of the cell. The largest and longest human muscle fibers are up to 30 centimeters long and 0.05 to 0.15 millimeter wide and contain several thousand nuclei.

Filling the inside of a muscle fiber, the myofibrils are the same length as the fiber and are the part that causes the cell to contract forcefully in response to

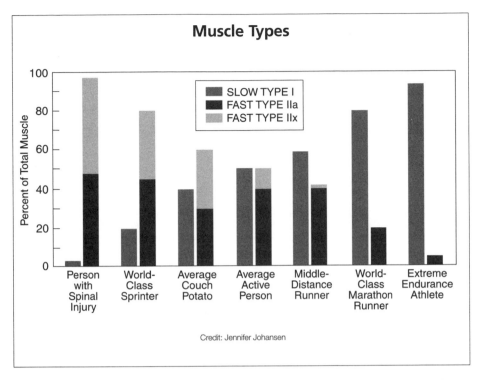

Muscle Types

Percent of Total Muscle

SLOW TYPE I
FAST TYPE IIa
FAST TYPE IIx

Person with Spinal Injury
World-Class Sprinter
Average Couch Potato
Average Active Person
Middle-Distance Runner
World-Class Marathon Runner
Extreme Endurance Athlete

Credit: Jennifer Johansen

nerve impulses. Motor nerve cells, or neurons, extend from the spinal cord to a group of fibers, making up a motor unit. In leg muscles, a motor neuron controls, or "innervates," several hundred to 1,000 or more muscle fibers. Where extreme precision is needed, for example, to control a finger, an eyeball or the larynx, one motor neuron controls only one or at most a few muscle fibers.

The actual contraction of a myofibril is accomplished by its tiny component units, which are called sarcomeres and are linked end to end to make up a myofibril. Within each sarcomere are two filamentary proteins, known as myosin and actin, whose interaction causes the contraction. Basically, during contraction a sarcomere shortens like a collapsing telescope, as the actin filaments at each end of a central myosin filament slide toward the myosin's center.

One component of the myosin molecule, the so-called heavy chain, determines the functional characteristics of the muscle fiber. In an adult, this heavy chain exists in three different varieties, known as isoforms. These isoforms are designated I, IIa and IIx, as are the fibers that contain them. Type I fibers are also known as slow fibers; type IIa and IIx are referred to as fast fibers. The fibers are called slow and fast for good reason: the maximum contraction velocity of a single type I fiber is approximately one tenth that of a type IIx fiber. The velocity of type IIa fibers is somewhere between those of type I and type IIx.

The Stuff of Muscle

The differing contraction speeds of the fibers is a result of differences in the way the fibers break down a molecule called adenosine triphosphate in the myosin heavy chain region to derive the energy needed for contraction. Slow fibers rely more on relatively efficient aerobic metabolism, whereas the fast fibers depend more on anaerobic metabolism. Thus, slow fibers are important for endurance activities and sports such as long-distance running, cycling and swimming, whereas fast fibers are key to power pursuits such as weight lifting and sprinting.

The "average" healthy adult has roughly equal numbers of slow and fast fibers in, say, the quadriceps muscle in the thigh. But as a species, humans show great variation in this regard; we have encountered people with a slow-fiber percentage as low as 19 percent and as high as 95 percent in the quadriceps muscle. A person with 95 percent slow fibers could probably become an accomplished marathoner but would never get anywhere as a sprinter; the opposite would be true of a person with 19 percent slow fibers.

Besides the three distinct fiber types, there are hybrids containing two different myosin isoforms. The hybrid fibers fall in a continuum ranging from those almost totally dominated by, say, the slow isoform to fibers almost totally dominated by a fast one. In either case, as might be expected, the functional characteristics of the fiber are close to those of the dominant fiber type.

Myosin is an unusual and intriguing protein. Comparing myosin isoforms from different mammals, researchers have found remarkably little variation from species to species. The slow (type I) myosin found in a rat is much more similar to the slow isoform found in humans than it is to the rat's own fast myosins. This fact suggests that selective evolutionary pressure has maintained functionally distinct myosin isoforms and that this pressure has basically preserved particular isoforms that came about over millions of years of evolution. These myosin types arose quite early in evolution—even the most ancient and primitive creatures had myosin isoforms not terribly different from ours.

Bulking Up

Muscle fibers cannot split themselves to form completely new fibers. As people age, they lose muscle fibers, but they never gain new ones [see box on pages 56–57]. So a muscle can become more massive only when its individual fibers become thicker.

What causes this thickening is the creation of additional myofibrils. The mechanical stresses that exercise exerts on tendons and other structures connected to the muscle trigger signaling proteins that activate genes that cause the muscle fibers to make more contractile proteins. These proteins, chiefly myosin and actin, are needed as the fiber produces great amounts of additional myofibrils.

More nuclei are required to produce and support the making of additional protein and to keep up a certain ratio of cell volume to nuclei. As mentioned, muscle fibers have multiple nuclei, but the nuclei within the muscle fiber cannot divide, so the new nuclei are donated by so-called satellite cells (also known as stem cells). Scattered among the many nuclei on the surface of a skeletal muscle fiber, satellite cells are largely separate from the muscle cell. The satellite cells have only one nucleus apiece and can replicate by dividing. After fusion with the muscle fiber, they serve as a source of new nuclei to supplement the growing fiber.

Satellite cells proliferate in response to the wear and tear of exercise. One theory holds that rigorous exercise inflicts tiny "microtears" in muscle fibers. The damaged area attracts the satellite cells, which incorporate themselves into the muscle tissue and begin producing proteins to fill the gap. As the satellite cells multiply, some remain as satellites on the fiber, but others become incorporated into it. These nuclei become indistinguishable from the muscle cell's other nuclei. With these additional nuclei, the fiber is able to churn out more proteins and create more myofibrils.

To produce a protein, a muscle cell—like any cell in the body—must have a "blueprint" to specify the order in which amino acids should be put together to make the protein—in other words, to indicate which protein will be created. This blueprint is a gene in the cell's nucleus, and the process by which the information gets out of the nucleus into the cytoplasm, where the protein will be made, starts with transcription. It occurs in the nucleus when a gene's information (encoded in DNA) is copied into a molecule called messenger RNA. The mRNA then carries this information outside the nucleus to the ribosomes, which assemble amino acids into the proteins—actin or one of the myosin isoforms, for example—as specified by the mRNA. This last process is called translation. Biologists refer to the entire process of producing a protein from a gene as "expression" of that gene.

Two of the most fundamental areas of study in skeletal muscle research— ones that bear directly on athletic performance—revolve around the way in which exercise and other stimuli cause muscles to become enlarged (a process called hypertrophy) and how such activity can convert muscle fibers from one type to another. We and others have pursued these subjects intensively in recent years and have made some significant observations.

The research goes back to the early 1960s, when A. J. Buller and John Carew Eccles of the Australian National University in Canberra and later Michael Bárány and his co-workers at the Institute for Muscle Disease in New York City performed a series of animal studies that converted skeletal muscle fibers from fast to slow and from slow to fast. The researchers used several different means to convert the fibers, the most common of which was cross-innervation. They switched a nerve that controlled a slow muscle with one linked to a fast muscle, so that each controlled the opposite type of fiber. The researchers also electrically stimulated muscles for prolonged periods or, to get the opposite effect, cut the nerve leading to the muscle.

In the 1970s and 1980s muscle specialists focused on demonstrating that the ability of a muscle fiber to change size and type, a feature generally referred to as muscle plasticity, also applied to humans. An extreme example of this effect occurs in people who have suffered a spinal cord injury serious enough to have paralyzed their lower body. The lack of nerve impulses and general disuse of the muscle cause a tremendous loss of tissue, as might be expected. More surprisingly, the type of muscle changes dramatically. These paralyzed subjects experience a sharp decrease of the relative amount of the slow myosin isoform, whereas the amount of the fast myosin isoforms actually increases.

We have shown that many of these subjects have almost no slow myosin in their vastus lateralis muscle, which is part of the quadriceps in the thigh, after five to 10 years of paralysis; essentially all myosin in this muscle is of the fast type. Recall that in the average healthy adult the distribution is about

50–50 for slow and fast fibers. We hypothesized that the neural input to the muscle, by electrical activation, is necessary for maintaining the expression of the slow myosin isoform. Thus, electrical stimulation or electrically induced exercise of these subjects' muscles can, to some extent, reintroduce the slow myosin in the paralyzed muscles.

Converting Muscle

Conversion of muscle fibers is not limited to the extreme case of the reconditioning of paralyzed muscle. In fact, when healthy muscles are loaded heavily and repeatedly, as in a weight-training program, the number of fast IIx fibers declines as they convert to fast IIa fibers. In those fibers the nuclei stop expressing the IIx gene and begin expressing the IIa. If the vigorous exercise continues for about a month or more, the IIx muscle fibers will completely transform to IIa fibers. At the same time, the fibers increase their production of proteins, becoming thicker.

In the early 1990s Geoffrey Goldspink of the Royal Free Hospital in London suggested that the fast IIx gene constitutes a kind of "default" setting. This hypothesis has held up in various studies over the years that have found that sedentary people have higher amounts of myosin IIx in their muscles than do fit, active people. Moreover, complementary studies have found a positive correlation between myosin IIa and muscle activity.

What happens when exercise stops? Do the additional IIa fibers then convert back to IIx? The answer is yes, but not in the precise manner that might be expected. To study this issue, we took muscle samples (biopsies) from the vastus lateralis muscle of nine young, sedentary Danish men. We then had the subjects conduct heavy resistance training, aimed mainly at their quadriceps

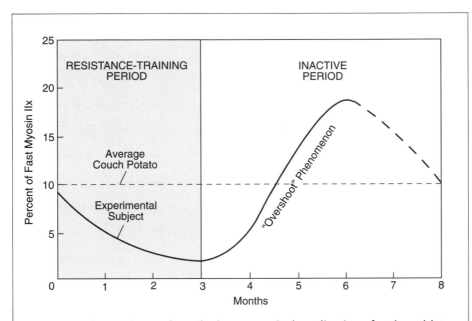

Unexpected experimental results have practical applications for the athlete. The fast IIx myosin declined as expected during resistance training. But when training stopped, rather than simply returning to the pretraining level, the relative amount of IIx roughly doubled three months into detraining. So what does this mean for the sprinter, to whom IIx is crucial? Provide for a period of reduced training before a competition.

Credit: Jennifer Johansen

muscle, for three months, ending with another muscle biopsy. Then the subjects abruptly stopped the resistance training and returned to their sedentary lifestyle, before being biopsied for a third and final time after a three-month period of inactivity (corresponding to their behavior prior to entering the training).

As expected, the relative amount of the fast myosin IIx isoform in their vastus lateralis muscle was reduced from an average of 9 percent to about 2 percent in the resistance-training period. We then expected that the relative amount of the IIx isoform would simply return to the pretraining level of 9 percent during the period of inactivity. Much to our surprise, the relative amount of myosin IIx reached an average value of 18 percent three months into the detraining. We did not continue the biopsies after the three-month period, but we strongly suspect that the myosin IIx did eventually return to its initial value of about 9 percent some months later.

We do not yet have a good explanation for this "overshoot" phenomenon of the expression of the fast myosin IIx isoform. Nevertheless, we can draw some conclusions that can have useful applications. For instance, if sprinters want to boost the relative amount of the fastest fibers in their muscles, the best strategy would be to start by removing those that they already have and then slow down the training and wait for the fastest fibers to return twofold! Thus, sprinters would be well advised to provide in their schedule for a period of reduced training, or "tapering," leading up to a major competition. In fact, many sprinters have settled on such a regimen simply through experience, without understanding the underlying physiology.

Slow to Fast?

Conversion between the two fast fiber types, IIa and IIx, is a natural consequence of training and detraining. But what about conversion between the slow and fast fibers, types I and II? Here the results have been somewhat murkier. Many experiments performed over the past couple of decades found no evidence that slow fibers can be converted to fast, and vice versa. But in the early 1990s we did get an indication that a rigorous exercise regimen could convert slow fibers to fast IIa fibers.

Our subjects were very elite sprinters, whom we studied during a three-month period in which they combined heavy resistance training with short-interval running (these are the foundation exercises in a sprinter's yearly training cycle). At around the same time, Mona Esbörnsson and her co-workers at the Karolinska Institute in Stockholm reported similar findings in a study involving a dozen subjects who were not elite athletes. These results suggest that a program of vigorous weight training supplemented with other forms of anaerobic exercise converts not only type IIx fibers to IIa but also type I fibers to IIa.

If a certain type of exertion can convert some type I fibers to IIa, we might naturally wonder if some other kind can convert IIa to I. It may be possible, but so far no lengthy human training study has unambiguously demonstrated such a shift. True, star endurance athletes such as long-distance runners and swimmers, cyclists and cross-country skiers generally have remarkably high proportions—up to 95 percent, as mentioned earlier—of the slow type I fibers in their major muscle groups, such as the legs. Yet at present we do not know whether these athletes were born with such a high percentage of type I fibers and gravitated toward sports that take advantage of their unusual inborn trait or whether they very gradually increased the proportion of type I fibers in their muscles as they trained over a period of many months or years. We do know that if fast type IIa fibers can be converted to type I, the time required for the conversion is quite long in comparison with the time for the shift from IIx to IIa.

It may be that great marathon runners are literally born different from other people. Sprinters, too, might be congenitally unusual: in contrast with long-distance runners, they of course would benefit from a relatively small percentage of type I fibers. Still, a would-be sprinter with too many type I fibers need not give up. Researchers have found that hypertrophy from resistance training enlarges type II fibers twice as much as it does type I fibers. Thus, weight training can increase the cross-sectional area of the muscle covered by fast fibers without changing the relative ratio between the number of slow and fast fibers in the muscle. Moreover, it is the relative cross-sectional area of the fast and slow fibers that determines the functional characteristics of the entire muscle. The more area covered by fast fibers, the faster the over-all muscle will be. So a sprinter at least has the option of altering the characteristics of his or her leg muscles by exercising them with weights to increase the relative cross section of fast fibers.

In a study published in 1988 Michael Sjöström and his co-workers at the University of Umea, Sweden, disclosed their finding that the average cross-sectional areas of the three main fiber types were almost identical in the vas-tus lateralis muscles of a group of marathon runners. In those subjects the cross-sectional area of type I fibers averaged 4,800 square microns; type IIa was 4,500; and type IIx was 4,600. For a group of sprinters, on the other hand, the average fiber sizes varied considerably: the type I fibers averaged 5,000 square microns; type IIa, 7,300; and type IIx, 5,900. We have results from a group of sprinters that are very similar.

Although certain types of fiber conversion, such as IIa to I, appear to be difficult to bring about through exercise, the time is fast approaching when researchers will be able to accomplish such conversions easily enough through genetic techniques. Even more intriguing, scientists will be able to trigger the expression of myosin genes that exist in the genome but are not normally expressed in human muscles. These genes are like archival blue-prints for myosin types that might have endowed ancient mammalian rela-tives of ours with very fast muscle tissue that helped them escape predators, for example.

Such genetic manipulations, most likely in the form of vaccines that insert artificial genes into the nuclei of muscle cells, will almost certainly be the performance-enhancing drugs of the future. Throughout the recorded history of sports a persistent minority of athletes have abused performance-enhancing substances. Organizations such as the International Olympic Committee have for decades tried to suppress these drugs by testing athletes and censuring those found to have cheated. But as soon as new drugs are invented, they are co-opted by dishonest athletes, forcing officials to develop new tests. The result has been an expensive race pitting the athletes and their "doctors" against the various athletic organizations and the scientists developing new antidoping tests.

This contest is ongoing even now in Sydney, but within the near future, when athletes can avail themselves of gene therapy techniques, they will have taken the game to a whole new level. The tiny snippets of genetic material and the proteins that gene therapy will leave behind in the athletes' muscle cells may be impossible to identify as foreign.

Gene therapy is now being researched intensively in most developed countries—for a host of very good reasons. Instead of treating deficiencies by injecting drugs, doctors will be able to prescribe genetic treatments that will induce the body's own protein-making machinery to produce the proteins needed to combat illness. Such strategies became possible, at least in theory, in recent years as researchers succeeded in making artificial copies of the human genes that could be manipulated to produce large amounts of specific proteins. Such genes can be introduced into the human body where, in many cases, they substitute for a defective gene.

Like ordinary genes, the artificial gene consists of DNA. It can be delivered to the body in several ways. Suppose the gene encodes for one of the many signaling proteins or hormones that stimulate muscle growth. The direct approach would be to inject the DNA into the muscle. The muscle fibers would then take up the DNA and add it to the normal pool of genes.

This method is not very efficient yet, so researchers often use viruses to carry the gene payload into a cell's nuclei. A virus is essentially a collection of genes packed in a protein capsule that is able to bind to a cell and inject the genes. Scientists replace the virus's own genes with the artificial gene, which the virus will then efficiently deliver to cells in the body.

Unfortunately, and in contrast to the direct injection of DNA, the artificial gene payload will be delivered not only to the muscle fibers but also to many other cells, such as those of the blood and the liver. Undesirable side effects could very well occur when the artificial gene is expressed in cell types other than the targeted ones. For example, if a gene causing extended muscle hypertrophy were injected, this would lead to the desired growth of the skeletal muscles. But it would probably also lead to hypertrophy of another kind of muscle, namely that of the heart, giving rise to all the well-known complications of having an enlarged heart. So researchers have explored another approach, which entails removing specific cell types from the patient, adding the artificial gene in the laboratory and reintroducing the cells into the body.

These techniques will be abused by athletes in the future. And sports officials will be hard-pressed to detect the abuse, because the artificial genes will produce proteins that in many cases are identical to the normal proteins. Furthermore, only one injection will be needed, minimizing the risk of disclosure. It is true that officials will be able to detect the DNA of the artificial gene itself, but to do so they would have to know the sequence of the artificial gene, and the testers would have to obtain a sample of the tissue containing the DNA. Athletes, of course, will be quite reluctant to surrender muscle samples before an important competition. Thus, a doping test based on taking pieces of the athletes' muscle is not likely to become routine. For all intents and purposes, gene doping will be undetectable.

Brave New World

What will athletics be like in an age of genetic enhancements? Let us reconsider our opening scenario, at the men's 100-meter final. Only this time it is the year 2012. Prior to these Olympics, it was hard to pick an obvious favorite for the gold medal. After the preliminary heats, that is not so anymore. Already after the semifinals the bookmakers closed the bets for the runner in lane four, John Doeson. He impressed everyone by easing through his ⅛ final in a time only $\frac{3}{100}$ of a second from the now eight-year-old world record. In the quarterfinal he broke the world record by $\frac{15}{100}$ of a second, but the 87,000 spectators did not believe their eyes when in the semifinals he lowered the world record to an unbelievable 8.94 seconds, passing the finish line more than 10 meters ahead of the second-place runner. This performance made several television commentators maintain that the viewers had just seen "something from out of this world."

Not quite, but close. What could have led to such an astonishing performance? By 2012 gene therapy will probably be a well-established and widely used medical technology. Let us say that 12 months before the Olympics, a doctor approached Doeson with a proposal likely to sorely tempt any sprinter. What if you could make your muscle cells express the fastest myosin isoform? Under normal conditions, this isoform is not expressed in any of the major human skeletal muscles, but the gene is there and ready to work, like a dusty blueprint that just needs a civil engineer and a construction crew to make it a reality.

This enticing myosin isoform would give muscle fibers functional characteristics that correspond to those of the very fast IIb isoform, found in the rat and in other small mammals that need bursts of speed to elude predators. This IIb isoform has a much higher velocity of contraction and so can generate more power than IIx or IIa fibers. Although Doeson didn't really understand

Muscle and the Elderly

Everyone knows that when we age, our muscles weaken and our movements become slower. But why is that so? With aging come a number of changes to the skeletal muscles. Most marked is the loss of mass, which begins as early as 25 years of age. By age 50 the skeletal muscle mass is often reduced by 10 percent, and by age 80 approximately 50 percent of the muscle mass is gone.

This age-related reduction is caused mainly by a loss of muscle fibers. By greatly thickening the individual fibers, weight lifting can stave off the loss of mass from the muscle as a whole, but it appears to have no major effect on the loss of fibers.

Before individual fibers are lost to atrophy, they change shape and appearance. In young people, muscle fibers are distinctively angular, whereas in the elderly they often appear more rounded and in extreme cases banana-shaped. Furthermore, aging seems to induce "type grouping": in young and middle-aged skeletal muscle the fast and slow fibers are distributed in a chessboard fashion, whereas in aged muscle the fibers cluster in groups of either slow or fast cells (this phenomenon also appears in younger people suffering from certain motor nerve–related diseases).

The findings have prompted some researchers to hypothesize that fiber types cluster in elderly muscle as a consequence of a complex process in which the muscle-controlling nerves switch from one muscle fiber to another. Consider the motor unit, defined as all the muscle fibers controlled, or "innervated," by a single motor nerve originating from the spinal cord. As we age, some of these motor nerves "die." The nerve's muscle fibers are then left without any input, so they, too, atrophy and die—unless they are reinnervated by another motor nerve.

Intriguingly, if a muscle fiber is reinnervated by a nerve from a different motor unit type—for example, if a fast muscle fiber is reinnervated by a nerve from slow fibers—the fiber will be left with conflicting signals. Developmentally it is a fast fiber, but it receives stimulation that leads to an activation pattern that fits a slow fiber. Ultimately, this change in stimulation appears to transform the fast fiber to a slow fiber (or vice versa, in the opposite case).

Aging appears to be harder on the fast fibers, which atrophy at a higher rate than the slow ones do. So some researchers have long suspected that the distribution of fast and slow fibers gradually shifts as we age to favor the slow fibers. This, they reasoned, could help explain why a 10-year-old boy will outrun his 70-year-old grandfather in a 100-meter race, whereas Grandpa might still defeat Junior in a 10K.

The hypothesis is somewhat controversial because it has been difficult to prove that aging leads to an increase in the relative amount of slow fibers. In a recent study, we set out to approach the problem a little differently. We persuaded a group of 12 elderly and frail subjects with an average age of 88 years to submit to a muscle biopsy from their vastus lateralis muscle (which is located on the front side of the thigh and is one of the most well examined of human skeletal muscles).Then, working with thin needles under a microscope, we dissected out single muscle fibers from the tissue samples. We determined the myosin isoform composition of each of 2,300 single fibers.

We know that all humans have not only pure slow and fast fibers but also fibers that contain both the slow and the IIa (fast) myosin isoforms or both fast isoforms (IIa and IIx). In the young vastus lateralis muscle these hybrid fibers are scarce: fewer than 5 percent of the fibers contain both the slow myosin I and fast myosin IIa isoform. In our elderly subjects we found that a third of all the examined fibers contained these two myosin isoforms. Astonishingly, this hybrid fiber was the predominant type in the very aged muscle.

We concluded that the question of whether aging muscle has more slow fibers cannot be answered with a simple yes or no. What seems to happen is not a change in ratio between slow and fast fibers but more an obfuscation of the border between slow and fast fibers, so that in very elderly muscle one third of the fibers are neither strictly slow nor fast but rather somewhere in between.

what the doctor was talking about, he fully understood the words "velocity" and "power."

The doctor enthusiastically went on explaining his idea. The gene actually expresses a kind of protein known as a transcription factor, which in turn activates the gene for the very fast myosin IIb isoform. Such a transcription factor was discovered a few years ago and was named Velociphin. Holding a tiny glass vial in front of Doeson's face, he intoned: "This is the DNA for an artificial gene for Velociphin. Just a few injections of this DNA into your quadriceps, hamstring and gluteus, and your muscle fibers will start cranking out Velociphin, which will activate the myosin IIb gene."

Within three months, he added, Doeson's muscles would contain a good portion of IIb fibers, enabling him to break the 100-meter world record with ease. Moreover, the doctor noted, Doeson's muscles would keep producing Velociphin for years without further injections. And without a muscle biopsy from the quadriceps, hamstring or gluteus, there will be no way for officials to detect the genetic modification.

A year later, as he pulls on his track suit, Doeson recalls the doctor's assurance that there would be no side effects of the genetic treatment. So far, so good. After stretching and warming up, he takes his place on the block in lane four. "On your mark. Get set. BANG!" The runners are away.

A couple of seconds later Doeson is already ahead by two meters. Over the next few seconds, astonishingly, his lead grows. In comparison with those of the other runners, his strides are visibly more powerful and frequent. He feels good as he passes 30, 40 and 50 meters. But then, at 65 meters, far out in front of the field, he feels a sudden twinge in his hamstring. At 80 meters the twinge explodes into overwhelming pain as he pulls his hamstring muscle. A tenth of a second later Doeson's patella tendon gives in, because it is no match for the massive forces generated by his quadriceps muscle. The patella tendon pulls out part of the tibia bone, which then snaps, and the entire quadriceps shoots up along the femur bone. Doeson crumples to the ground, his running career over.

That is not the scenario that generally springs to mind in connection with the words "genetically engineered super-athlete." And some athletes will probably manage to exploit engineered genes while avoiding catastrophe. But it is clear that as genetic technologies begin trickling into the mainstream of medicine they will change sports profoundly—and not for the better. As a society, we will have to ask ourselves whether new records and other athletic triumphs really are a simple continuation of the age-old quest to show what our species can do.

Scientific American, September 2000

The Chemical Games

Biotechnical advances and administrative loopholes enable devious athletes to take performance-enhancing drugs without much risk of being caught or sanctioned

GLENN ZORPETTE

At this year's Olympic Games, a decades-old tradition will play out between the lighting of the torch and the closing ceremonies. This will be the testing of the urine, in which scientists armed with millions of dollars' worth of state-of-the-art instruments will look for obscure molecules in incredibly small concentrations signaling the recent use of one or more banned performance-enhancing drugs.

Unless a superstar athlete is caught cheating, not many spectators will give more than a passing thought to this behind-the-scenes struggle. But as surely as athletes will pit themselves against one another, some will also match wits with doctors, technicians and sports officials. A few athletes will probably be caught, triggering an appeal and arbitration process that will unfold well away from the public eye and under the aegis of officials with little or no formal education in physiology, pharmacology, or indeed any branch of science or medicine.

Even more dispiriting, it is a virtual certainty that a larger number of cheating athletes will beat the tests. Many of them will use a drug that cannot now be detected in urine. Others will carefully schedule and limit their use of banned substances so that their biochemical indicators will be below the thresholds that the International Olympic Committee (IOC) interprets as a damning result. If the previous Olympics are a guide, some athletes will even take drugs, be caught and then have their sanctions overturned by an arbitration process that tends to exonerate all but the most poorly informed and reckless cheaters.

Given the variety of ways to circumvent drug tests, officials are at a loss to say even how widely abused some of the substances are. But scattered evidence suggests troubling pervasiveness, at least in some sports and among certain teams. "If this were a basketball game, we'd be behind about 98 to 2," says a former high-ranking official of the U.S. Olympic Committee (USOC), who asked not to be identified. Moreover, drug use by a small minority can fatally undermine the fundamental precept of athletic competition, in which victory goes to the contestant who best combines such attributes as strength, coordination, endurance, discipline and cunning.

"Sport is well aware it is losing the battle," says Don H. Catlin, director of the Olympic Analytical Laboratory at the University of California at Los Angeles. "Sports officials are terribly concerned about this matter. It tears at them."

The pall of drug use has grown darker in recent years as evidence has accrued that athletes in a variety of sports are increasingly turning to erythropoietin (EPO) and human growth hormone (hGH), both relatively recent arrivals in the world of sports. Like hundreds of other substances explicitly banned by the IOC, these two are effective and easy to obtain. They have surged in popularity because, unlike the other agents, EPO and hGH are undetectable with the technology that sports officials currently use to catch transgressors.

A Brief History of Cheating

EPO and hGH are just the latest gambits in a cat-and-mouse game that is more than four decades old. By 1954 some Olympic weight lifters in the Soviet Union and elsewhere were using muscle-building anabolic steroids, according to sports historians. The chemical games had begun: the cheaters were in the lead, and their opponents have never caught up. As the pharmaceutical industry blossomed, new forms of steroids, stimulants, hormones and red blood cell growth hormones flowed into the market. Most of the substances spur muscle growth; a few improve endurance; still others, known as beta blockers, slow the heartbeat, which lets sharpshooters or archers take steadier aim and helps a figure skater calm jangled nerves before a big performance.

Today the dishonest athlete can choose from an assortment of about 36 different anabolic steroids (among them a couple originally intended for veterinary use). Athletes get the drugs in different ways, and some observers maintain that it is not terribly difficult for an elite athlete to find a sports physician who is willing to break professional rules to assist an Olympian on a quest to glorify his or her country.

Cheating athletes have tapped biotechnological bounty with impressive swiftness and sophistication. Meanwhile the Olympic movement, along with all of international sport, has been turning to ever more advanced technologies in concerted if sporadic attempts to catch them. "It's almost like the cold war was," says David Joyner, chair of the USOC's sports medicine committee.

Formal drug testing for stimulants began at the Mexico City Olympic Games in 1968, a year after a British cyclist who had taken stimulants died of heart failure while competing in a televised stage of the Tour de France and eight years after several cyclists perished suddenly and similarly at the 1960 Olympics in Rome.

Not until 1975 did the IOC finally ban muscle-building anabolic steroids. Seven years later it added testosterone and caffeine to its list of forbidden substances. Testosterone, a key male hormone, plays an important role in muscle building. Anabolic steroids are just synthetic versions of testosterone, tweaked so they can be taken orally or so that they persist in the body.

A sensitive, reliable test for the anabolic agents did not debut until 1983, at the Pan American Games in Caracas, Venezuela. A German physician set up a lab in which the primary instruments were gas chromatographs married to mass spectrometers. The chromatograph in one of these combined units is basically an elaborate discriminator: it takes a sample that has been vaporized and separates it into its component substances. The spectrometer then weighs the fragments to identify the specific molecule they came from. The instrument, known as a GCMS, is the workhorse technology that testers rely on to this day.

The use of the new technology in Caracas was not announced in advance to the competitors. As a result, 19 athletes tested positive for drugs at those games. More telling, many athletes—including a huge U.S. contingent—refused to be tested and left without competing. The next year, in 1984, GCMS was used for the first time in Olympic competition at the Los Angeles Games.

Sports officials, notably from East Germany and the Soviet Union (and subsequently Russia), were only mildly inconvenienced by the improved technology. Countries continued to operate elaborate programs that chemically enhanced hundreds or thousands of athletes and won hundreds of medals. At the 1988 Olympics in Seoul, for example, the Russian delegation reportedly operated a drug lab on board a ship docked in the harbor. The lab monitored Russian athletes to make sure they would not test positive for any banned substances. (Athletes on steroids simply stop taking them a few weeks prior to competition; continuing to exercise vigorously can retain for weeks the extra muscle mass.)

Members of the U.S. Olympic team, too, have been the subjects of disturbing allegations. Pat Connolly, a former U.S. Olympic women's track coach, told a Senate hearing in April 1989 that she believed that "at least 40 percent of the [U.S.] women's team in Seoul had probably used steroids at some time in their preparation for the games." It is worth noting that none of them tested positive in Seoul.

Although testers had a breakthrough at the 1984 Los Angeles Games with the GCMS, cheaters also made a major leap forward: blood doping. Weeks before the competition, eight of the 24 members of the U.S. cycling team had some of their blood removed and preserved. Their blood supply rebounded naturally over time. Shortly before competing they met in a southern California hotel and had their store of red blood cells transfused back into their system. Raising their red blood cell counts to abnormally high levels enabled their circulatory systems to carry more oxygen and thus improved their endurance considerably. The team went on to win a record nine medals before the doping was discovered, months later.

EPO: The Modern Era Begins

Blood doping had begun years earlier, but the old transfusion method is no longer used. The practice became considerably more convenient when EPO became available in the late 1980s. A peptide hormone that stimulates the production of red blood cells in bone marrow, EPO is found naturally in the body. In 1985 the biotechnology firm Amgen introduced EPO produced by recombinant means to treat kidney dialysis patients and others.

Too much of a good thing, however, can be fatal. EPO has been blamed for the deaths of about 20 European cyclists since 1988. Although there is no hard proof that EPO caused the deaths, some doping experts believe the riders' blood may have thickened and clotted fatally after they took too much of the drug.

The full magnitude of the EPO problem, at least in cycling, became apparent for the first time during the 1998 Tour de France, cycling's premier event. During the race, police officers found cases of the drug in car trunks and in the hotel rooms of many cyclists. Seven teams were implicated; one withdrew, and another was expelled.

Today, despite more than a decade of sporadic research and development, several million dollars spent and intermittent promises by sports organizations, there is still no test that directly identifies the presence of EPO. Before major races, however, officials in cycling (and also in cross-country skiing) routinely test blood samples from all competitors. Those with a hematocrit, or red blood cell percentage, higher than 50 are banned from the race. A normal hematocrit is around 42. The policy has so far prevented any more EPO-related fatalities during races, but it has done little to eliminate the drug from the cycling circuit. For example, the policy was in effect during the scandalous 1998 Tour de France, in which many dozens of riders are known to have used the drug.

Athletes in muscle sports such as weight lifting, sprinting, wrestling and short-distance swimming have their own options for obtaining an undetectable edge. Because hGH and testosterone are, like EPO, found naturally in the body, they can add muscle without leaving any incriminating molecules behind for the GCMS operators.

HGH is an astoundingly expensive steroid substitute. Yet its use was apparently rampant enough in Atlanta in 1996 to inspire some athletes to dub those Olympics the "hGH Games." Around that time, a Latvian company was doing brisk business harvesting hGH from human cadavers and selling it for athletic use. And as recently as February [2000], police in Oslo apprehended two Lithuanians with 3,000 ampoules of black-market hGH, according to Gunnar Hermansson, chief inspector of the drugs unit of Sweden's National Criminal Intelligence Service. The cache was enough to supply about 100 athletes for a month.

Esters of testosterone are another essentially undetectable muscle builder. As their name implies, they consist of testosterone linked to an ester, both organic molecules. The ester acts to delay the loss from the body of the hormone, which would otherwise be metabolized in hours. In the body, neither the testosterone nor the ester arouses suspicion, because both are found there naturally.

Sports officials can, however, detect gross abuse of esters of testosterone. As part of a standard drug test, they examine the relative amounts in the athlete's urine of testosterone and epitestosterone, a hormone of uncertain function. In a normal Caucasian male, the ratio is about one to one. If the ratio is found to be six to one or greater, the IOC and other sports organizations declare the test positive and the athlete is sanctioned, unless he can prove that he is the rare (one in 2,000) male who has such a high ratio naturally.

The situation is far from ideal. Doping experts say that some athletes use transdermal patches and other controlled delivery methods to boost the level of testosterone in their blood significantly while staying below the six-to-one ratio. Another problem is that the current practice does not treat different races equally: on average, Asians have lower levels of testosterone than blacks or Caucasians do, so it is considerably more difficult for an Asian athlete to dope himself beyond the six-to-one limit.

The Cheater's Last Loophole

Even if sports officials decide to sanction an athlete based on an elevated testosterone ratio or some other test result, they are often stymied by a recourse that increasingly seems like the abusing athlete's ace in the hole: the adjudication process. Suppose an athlete wins an Olympic medal but then tests positive for a banned substance. If the IOC decides to strip the athlete of his medal, he can appeal to the Court of Arbitration for Sport. The court must then decide within 24 hours whether to uphold or overturn the sanction.

The court, set up in the mid-1980s, comprises representatives from the IOC, the National Olympic Committees (NOCs), the International Federations (IFs) and representatives of the athletes. The NOCs are the agencies that govern and coordinate a country's Olympic representation and help train its athletes (the USOC is an example). The IFs organize and oversee amateur competition in a specific sport. The one group of people the court has never seen fit to include are those with formal expertise or credentials in the pharmacology or physiology of performance-enhancing drugs.

In its short history the court has leaned toward exoneration, unless the case is simple and compelling in the extreme. In Atlanta, tests of seven athletes—among them two Russians who had won bronze medals—indicated that they had used a drug called Bromantan. The IOC, which now regards the drug as both a stimulant and a masking agent, decided to disqualify the athletes. The case went to the Court of Arbitration, where the athletes' attorneys contended that the Bromantan merely strengthened the athletes' immune systems and helped them deal with the heat of summer in Atlanta. The argument swayed the court enough for it to overturn the disqualification.

The case was important because it suggested to many observers that the burden would fall on the prosecution to prove each case beyond a reasonable doubt. "A lot of people seem to have decided that the criminal standard is the one that should apply," says Larry D. Bowers, head of the drug-testing laboratory at the Indiana University School of Medicine. Unfortunately for prosecutors, the complexity of the biochemical evidence often leaves defense attorneys enough room to generate at least a trace of doubt in adjudicators' minds.

Banned Performance Enhancers and Their Effects

The International Olympic Committee bans drugs in several categories.
A few examples from each group, and their most common side effects, appear here.

Drug	Benefits	Side Effects	Notes
Stimulants			
Amphetamine, methamphetamine	Increases endurance; relieves fatigue; improves reaction times	Irregular heartbeat, false sense of well-being, irritability, nervousness, restlessness, trouble sleeping	Used to treat narcolepsy and Attention Deficit Hyperactivity Disorder
Caffeine	Increases alertness; reduces drowsiness; promotes endurance	Nervousness, irritability, sleeplessness, diarrhea, dizziness, fast heartbeat, nausea, tremors, vomiting	Brewed coffee per cup contains 40–180 milligrams; illegal urine levels are 12 micrograms per milliliter
Pseudoephedrine	In high doses, acts like amphetamines; narrows blood vessels	Increases blood pressure in patients who have high blood pressure	Decongestant (narrowing blood vessels decreases nasal congestion)
Salbutamol (albuterol)	Controls "bronchospasms" induced by exercise; opens up the lungs' bronchial tubes	Fast heartbeat, headache, nervousness, trembling	Used to treat or prevent symptoms of asthma, chronic bronchitis, emphysema and other lung diseases
Anabolic Steroids			
Androstenediol, androstenedione, 19-norandrostenediol, 19-norandrostenedione, nandrolone, stanozolol, testosterone	Increases strength, muscle mass and aggressiveness	Acne or oily skin, enlarged clitoris/penis, deepened voice, unusual hair loss or growth, psychological disturbances; in sexually mature males, enlarged breasts	Androstenedione is available over the counter in the U.S. but is illegal in most other countries
Clenbuterol	Increases strength and muscle mass	Tremors and heart palpitations (tachycardia)	Decreases exercise capacity in rats, presumably due to changed cardiac muscle structure and function

Compiled by Naomi Lubick. Sources: International Olympic Committee; Don H. Catlin, University of California at Los Angeles; Larry Bowers, University of Illinois; Mayo Clinic; National Institutes of Health.

Diuretics

Acetazolamide	Increases urine flow and volume; prevents or lessens high-altitude effects	Unusual tiredness or weakness, diarrhea, general discomfort, loss of appetite or weight loss	Anticonvulsant (for epilepsy); used to treat glaucoma
Bumetanide, chlorthalidone, hydrochlorothiazide, triamterene	Increases urine flow and volume, diluting drugs or decreasing weight for sports with weight categories	Makes skin more sensitive to sunlight	Used to treat high blood pressure (hypertension) or to lower the amount of water in the body

Masking Agents

Bromantan	Supposedly masks the use of other drugs, presumably steroids	Unknown	Russian-developed "immunostimulator"; unavailable in West
Probenecid	Stops excretion of steroids for a few hours, decreasing urine steroid concentration	Headache, joint pain, redness or swelling, loss of appetite, nausea or vomiting (mild)	Used to treat chronic gout or gouty arthritis; improves functioning of penicillins

Peptide Hormones, Mimetics and Analogues

Chorionic gonadotropin (hCG)	Elevates testosterone production in men	Breast enlargement, headache, irritability; in women: bloating, stomach pain; in boys: acne, rapid increase in height, pubic hair growth, enlargement of testes and penis	Used by women to promote conception or in vitro fertilization and by men to produce testosterone
Human growth hormone (hGH)	Decreases fat mass; thought to improve human performance	Diabetes; abnormal growth of bones and internal organs such as the heart, liver and kidneys; atherosclerosis; high blood pressure (hypertension)	Used to treat growth disorders and prevent AIDS-related weight loss
Erythropoietin (EPO)	Increases circulating red blood cells, carrying more oxygen to muscles	Oily skin, acne and muscle tremors; thickens blood, increasing chances of stroke, myocardial infarction and heart failure	Used for treating anemia in patients with kidney disease, cancer and HIV
Beta Blockers Atenolol, bisoprolol, metoprolol, nadolol, propranolol	Slows heartbeat, enabling archers or shooters to increase their "interbeat interval"	Slows cardiac response time; makes running difficult; makes skin more sensitive to sun and temperature extremes	Used with a diuretic to treat high blood pressure

Getting through the Nets

Although it is undoubtedly nice to know it is there, an athlete-friendly adjudication process is something that most clever drug users will not need. Various administrative and logistical factors conspire to create holes in the nets set up to snare cheaters.

Because of its position at the pinnacle of amateur athletics, the IOC is often regarded as the central figure in high-stakes drug testing. In reality, the situation is far more complicated. The IOC is responsible for drug testing during the Olympic Games, but that is only a small fraction of the testing performed on elite amateur athletes. At each Olympics, the medal winners at every event submit urine samples at doping-control stations immediately following their events. One or two non-medalists are also generally tested at random. Athletes are selected arbitrarily, too, at preliminary events and from teams in final and semifinal rounds. In all, just under 20 percent of all athletes are tested during an Olympiad.

Officially, over the past 30 years only 52 athletes have been caught and sanctioned for using drugs in Olympic competition. Not even the staunchest Olympic booster thinks that only 52 athletes have cheated in the past three decades; it is now well known that far more than 52 competitors from the former East Germany alone took drugs and eluded detection. Even today the low rate of detection is thought to reflect the fact that the games are the one time when an athlete can be sure of being tested if he or she does well. "These days you have to be a total idiot to test positive at an event," says Bob Condron, a spokesman for the USOC.

This and other factors shift attention to the role of the IFs and the NOCs in drug testing. The IFs oversee drug tests at major non-Olympic competitions in the specific sports they administer. But it is the NOCs that arguably have the most crucial drug-testing role in all of amateur sports. They are responsible for testing athletes throughout their training—the period when almost all performance-enhancing substances, other than stimulants, are taken. The NOCs also test at national championships and at international competitions in their respective countries. Yet the world's many NOCs approach their drug-testing duties with varying degrees of rigor and vigilance.

Whereas tests by the IOC during Olympic Games are anticipated by athletes, the NOCs have the power to test athletes with little advance notice—or, ideally, no notice at all. Until recently, most NOCs have taken advantage of this opportunity relatively infrequently, if at all. And when they did, they often performed short-notice tests, in which the athlete was given 48 hours' warning that he or she would be tested. The tip-off would often enable a cheating athlete to take steps to expunge or mask the telltale chemicals. "A lot of athletes can clear their systems in 24 hours," explains Baaron Pittenger, head of the USOC's antidoping committee.

According to Catlin, athletes can try at least 13 different diuretics, which stimulate urination that dilutes incriminating chemicals and speeds them out of the body. A drug called probenecid has been used to interfere with the excretion of steroids. A few athletes, Catlin adds, have even endured the excruciatingly painful process of using a long needle to put untainted urine into their own bladder. Diuretics and probenecid are no longer as effective as they once were, because testers now routinely check for them.

Some NOCs are finally making more use of no-advance-notice tests. Joan Price, senior manager of drug testing for the USOC, says the organization performed 1,345 no-advance-notice tests in 1999, up from about 800 the previous year. It carried out 4,024 additional tests during competitions. For both the no-advance-notice tests and the ones performed during competitions, the rate of positive results was between 3 and 4 percent, she says.

The main reason why NOCs have been slow to pursue no-advance-notice testing more rigorously is that it is a relatively expensive, travel-intensive process. In some cases, it requires paying for a tester to travel hundreds or thousands of miles to meet an individual athlete.

Does the IOC Mean Business?

Although the NOCs have the power to be the main bulwark against the use of performance-enhancing drugs, the IOC remains firmly entrenched at the center of the antidrug movement. Some reasons are practical: the organization plays a key role in formulating drug-testing policy, sets the standards for drug-testing laboratories worldwide and is also the largest single source of funding for drug-testing research. Other reasons have more to do with perceptions. Because the IOC is the highest Olympic governing body, its moves in the fight against performance enhancement greatly influence how the broader Olympic movement regards the effort.

Unfortunately, the IOC's actions over the past two or three decades have repeatedly left observers questioning the organization's commitment. At Los Angeles in 1984, papers describing between five and nine positive drug tests were taken from a safe and shredded shortly after the end of the games. The athletes involved could therefore not even be identified, much less sanctioned. The records had been secured in a hotel room used by Prince Alexandre de Merode of Belgium, chair of the IOC's Medical Commission, which oversees antidrug activities. De Merode later said he believed the papers were taken mistakenly and destroyed by members of the Los Angeles Olympic Organizing Committee. (He declined repeated invitations from *Scientific American Presents* to be interviewed for this article.)

Months after the 1996 Atlanta Games, it came to light that four test results indicating use of the steroid methandienone were never acted on. The results were obtained with an extremely sophisticated high-resolution mass spectrometer (HRMS), which was being used for the first time during Olympic competition in Atlanta. The HRMS, which costs a cool $860,000, has about 10 times the resolution of a conventional GCMS. The greater sensitivity means that the high-resolution unit can often detect steroid metabolites in a urine sample more than a month after the athlete has stopped taking the drugs, as opposed to perhaps two or three weeks later with a conventional GCMS.

After the drug testers reported the four positive results to the IOC toward the end of the games, the IOC decided not to take action on them. Having been stung by the Bromantan experience just a few days before, the organization apparently decided it could not win a case based on evidence from a machine that some regarded as experimental.

Why would the IOC not want to vigorously root out and prosecute drug use at every opportunity? Some critics, including former athletes, have speculated that a large number of drug busts at an Olympics would undermine public support and enthusiasm for the games by tarnishing the sheen of fair competition. It is increasingly hard to accept that notion, though, given that the Tour de France has hardly suffered despite a scandal only two years ago that was about as bad as can be imagined.

What's Different Now?

As the Sydney Olympics get under way, a comparison between the current state of Olympic drug testing with what it was on the eve of the 1996 Atlanta Games is revealing—and perhaps a little depressing. The tests, technology and administrative procedures available to sports officials are essentially unchanged. And few antidrug officials were satisfied with the way things turned out in Atlanta. After all, these were the Olympics known as the hGH Games, in which 11 athletes are known to have tested positive for banned substances and suffered no consequences.

There may be one small but potentially significant technological advance for the antidrug forces. Officials may make more use of a technique known as carbon isotope ratio detection to determine whether competitors have taken synthetic testosterone. The test would be a vast improvement over the current method—the dubious search for a testosterone-to-epitestosterone ratio greater than six to one.

The carbon isotope ratio technique is telling because drug companies use plant sterols from soybeans to produce synthetic testosterone. Natural testosterone in the body comes from cholesterol. Compared with carbon atoms in natural testosterone, the carbon atoms in a sample of synthetic testosterone have a slightly lower ratio of the carbon 13 isotope to carbon 12. By measuring this ratio, researchers can determine if some of the carbon in a testosterone sample originated outside the body.

Researchers did have a carbon isotope ratio detection system in Atlanta and also at the 1998 Winter Games in Nagano, Japan, but the machines were used only experimentally. At press time, the IOC was evaluating whether it would incorporate the machine into its routine tests.

Whither Wada?

Even if there is a test for testosterone in Sydney, there will be none for the two other natural hormones, EPO and hGH. The reasons why are complex [see

"All Doped Up—and Going for the Gold," page 77]. The short, simplified answer is that the IOC, unwilling to put its full support behind experimental tests that might not withstand legal challenge in the Court of Arbitration, opted to plow its resources into a new antidrug bureaucracy, the World Anti-Doping Agency (WADA).

WADA was formed to bring together, for the purpose of fighting the spread of performance-enhancing drugs, representatives of the IOC, the IFs, the NOCs, Olympic athletes, 12 national governments, and bodies from various international organizations, such as the United Nations. Perhaps not coincidentally, its formation was announced to great fanfare in February 1999 as the reverberations from the Salt Lake City Olympics bribery scandal were reaching a crescendo at the IOC. WADA's director is Richard W. Pound, an attorney, a former Canadian Olympic swimmer and a longtime IOC vice president who is often mentioned as the favorite to succeed Juan Antonio Samaranch as IOC president.

According to Pound, the IOC has pledged to spend $25 million over two years to get WADA up and running. It hopes that by then ongoing contributions will be coming from additional sources, such as national governments and international organizations. In explaining the need for WADA, Pound notes that the fight against performance-enhancing drugs is now a sprawling effort, heavily dependent on the work of the NOCs, IFs and, in some cases, customs agents and national police forces. WADA will be a single place where all those parties can plot strategy and find common ground among their agendas. But getting so many agencies to cooperate will probably be more challenging than it might initially seem. Although antidrug efforts are decades-old, the Olympic movement, including the NOCs and the often recalcitrant IFs, agreed on a single, uniform antidoping code only this past

January. Pound also expects that with its diverse membership base, WADA will be able to assume a role as a larger, more effective platform for directing and funding research and development on drug tests.

It is possible, however, that drug-testing research as it is practiced today is nearing a twilight of sorts. In the near future dopers will take their perennial, escalating struggle with their keepers to a new level. Within a decade, perhaps, athletes will be able to inject themselves with genetic vaccines that will induce their body's own protein-making apparatus to add muscle mass or increase EPO (or both). In fact, in an overlooked experiment reported in 1997, Eric C. Svensson and others at the University of Chicago successfully used a genetic technique to boost the levels of EPO in the blood of some adult cynomolgus monkeys. The researchers subsequently measured hematocrits as high as 70 in the monkeys. (To keep the monkeys alive, the researchers diluted their blood.) When such genetic vaccines become available to athletes, the chemical games will be pretty much over. It will be difficult, if not impossible, for testers to distinguish inserted fragments of DNA from the DNA that was already there.

"When you come to a method where you are increasing proteins in the cells genetically and directly, you'll have to have much more sophisticated detection techniques," says Mats Garle, scientific director of the IOC-affiliated Doping Control Laboratory at Huddinge University Hospital in Sweden. After a moment's reflection, he admits, "Maybe we'll never get a solution to that problem."

Scientific American Presents: Building the Elite Athlete, Fall 2000

All Doped Up— and Going for the Gold

*Miscues by the International Olympic Committee
frustrate scientists developing tests for the
performance-enhancing drugs erythropoietin
and human growth hormone*

GLENN ZORPETTE

This coming September [2000], alongside the stirring spectacle of Olympic competition in Sydney, there will be another struggle so complex that the average viewer will probably have a hard time grasping the rules, let alone getting excited about it. Unfortunately, the loser will be fair competition.

The use of performance-enhancing drugs has long been one of the darkest aspects of sport, but the shadow has grown longer in recent years as evidence accrues that athletes are increasingly turning to two drugs relatively new on the doping scene: erythropoietin and human growth hormone. Like hundreds of other substances that are formally banned by the International Olympic Committee (IOC), these two are effective and fairly easy to get. Unlike the other agents, however, erythropoietin and human growth hormone are undetectable with the technology that sports officials currently use to catch drug cheats.

With sporadic funding from the IOC and other sources, researchers in half a dozen countries have been working feverishly over the past couple of years to come up with reliable tests for the two drugs. Unfortunately, although they have come tantalizingly close, the tests will probably not be ready in time for the Sydney games, several researchers say. More disturbing, scientists in three of the laboratories, in separate interviews, tell much the same story: they could have had the tests available for the games, but they were stymied by late decisions and a seeming lack of will at the highest levels of the IOC.

Without a reliable test, officials are at a loss even to say how widely abused the two drugs are. Scattered evidence suggests troubling pervasiveness, at least in some sports or among certain teams. "If this were a basketball game, we'd be behind about 98 to 2," remarks a former official of the U.S. Olympic Committee (USOC) who asked not to be identified.

Erythropoietin (EPO) is a hormone that occurs naturally in the body. Injected into the blood, it boosts the concentration of red cells and is favored by endurance athletes. It started catching on with competitors in the late 1980s, after a synthetic version was introduced to treat certain forms of kidney disease. Rigorous studies in Sweden and Australia have shown that EPO can improve an endurance athlete's performance by 7 to 10 percent.

In 1998 the Tour de France, the world's preeminent bicycle race, was thrown into disarray as investigators found caches of the drug in team vans, in car trunks and in the hotel rooms of competitors; a subsequent investigation concluded that use of the drug was endemic among cycling's elite. EPO is also blamed for the deaths of about 20 European riders since 1987. Although there is no hard proof that EPO caused the deaths, some doping experts believe the riders' blood thickened fatally after they took too much of the drug. Despite the 1998 scandal and the deaths, experts say EPO is still ubiquitous in cycling and is also widely used in cross-country skiing and long-distance running and swimming.

In contrast to EPO, human growth hormone (hGH) is a steroid-like agent that helps build muscle. Its use, however, may be just as widespread. In

1996 some athletes dubbed the Atlanta Olympics the "hGH Games." Around that time, a Latvian company was doing brisk business harvesting hGH from human cadavers and selling it for athletic use. In early 1998 a Chinese swimmer on her way to a competition in Perth was detained at the airport when she arrived with 13 vials of hGH packed in a thermos bottle. And just this past February 10, police in Oslo apprehended two Lithuanians harboring 3,000 ampoules of black-market hGH, according to Gunnar Hermansson, chief inspector of the drugs unit of Sweden's National Criminal Intelligence Service. The cache was enough to supply about 100 athletes for two months.

Reliable tests for EPO and hGH have eluded researchers for several reasons. The most imposing is that both substances are peptide hormones found naturally in the body. Thus, much of the research so far has focused on developing a so-called index test, in which an unusual combination of biological "markers" indicates drug use. The process would translate a variety of physiological parameters—for example, the concentration of red blood cells and the average age and size of the cells—into numerical values. If the combination of those values exceeded a certain number, officials could say with a high degree of certainty that the athlete had taken drugs.

The main project to develop the hGH test, at St. Thomas's Hospital in London, was suspended recently for lack of funding. According to Peter H. Sönksen, the project leader, his team had demonstrated by the end of 1998 a test that worked well on healthy Caucasian athletes. But he needed more funding to perform clinical trials to make sure the test worked with athletes of Asian and African descent, women taking birth-control pills, and athletes recovering from muscle injuries. "The estimated bill was $5 million," Sönksen says. "The IOC has decided not to invest further money to develop the test."

The IOC's decision is puzzling when considered in the context of the organization's other recent moves. Although the IOC apparently could not spare $5 million to finish the work on the hGH test, it did pledge early in 1999 to spend $25 million over two years to start a new antidrug bureaucracy, the World Anti-Doping Agency. Prince Alexandre de Merode of Belgium, chairman of the IOC's Medical Commission, which oversees antidrug activities, declined repeated invitations from *Scientific American* to explain the rationale behind the IOC's budgetary decisions.

Sönksen says he gave the IOC ample advance notice that in order for his test to be ready in time for Sydney, he would have to undertake a sizable crash program of clinical trials. "Prince de Merode had warning from August 1998 that this was going to happen," he maintains.

The IOC still funds EPO research, having pledged $1.25 million to scientists working on a test. The leading team working on the EPO test is an international consortium based at the Australian Sports Drug Testing Laboratory in Pymble, a suburb of Sydney; a smaller effort is also under way at the drug-testing laboratory at the University of California at Los Angeles. An Olympic official in the U.S. who requested anonymity but is familiar with the work in both laboratories says it is very unlikely that the EPO test will be ready in time for Sydney. A researcher in the Australian laboratory confirms that the chances of having a test ready are slim, adding, "If we'd got the money when we asked for it, the chances would have been a lot better."

Associates of de Merode—himself a former competitive cyclist—say the prince is keenly aware of the toll EPO has taken on his favorite sport. Nevertheless, the IOC may have been reluctant to spend more on the development of index tests, some experts speculate, because such tests detect drug use by indirect means and are therefore more vulnerable to legal challenge by athletes who have been sanctioned for doping. "The ability to shoot holes in the prosecution process is greatly diminished when you have a direct test," explains David Joyner, chairman of the USOC's sports medicine committee and vice chairman of its antidoping committee.

The French IOC doping laboratory in Paris is developing a direct test for EPO. But it will not be ready for a few years, and researchers familiar with the test say it will be able to detect foreign EPO only if administered within three days of an injection. EPO is typically injected one to three times a week for a month before a competition. So the direct test probably will be useful primarily for precompetition spot checks of athletes.

Although a direct test would nicely complement an indirect one, most officials agree that an indirect test alone would be far better than none. And other than drug cheats, no one is happy that yet another Olympic Games will apparently unfold under the distorting influence of two pervasive and powerful performance enhancers. "There's no question we should have tests for growth hormone and EPO," says Don H. Catlin, director of the U.C.L.A. lab. "Sport has the money to support R&D commensurate with assuring clean games. If we want to preserve sport as we know it, we're going to have to pay for it."

Scientific American, May 2000

Gene Doping

Gene therapy for restoring muscle lost to age or disease is poised to enter the clinic, but elite athletes are eyeing it to enhance performance. Can it be long before gene doping changes the nature of sport?

H. LEE SWEENEY

Athletes will be going to Athens next month [August 2004] to take part in a tradition begun in Greece more than 2,000 years ago. As the world's finest specimens of fitness test the extreme limits of human strength, speed and agility, some of them will probably also engage in a more recent, less inspiring Olympic tradition: using performance-enhancing drugs. Despite repeated scandals, doping has become irresistible to many athletes, if only to keep pace with competitors who are doing it. Where winning is paramount, athletes will

Overview: Molecular Muscle Building

- Muscle growth and repair are controlled by chemical signals, which are in turn controlled by genes. Muscle lost to age or disease can be replaced by boosting or blocking these signals with the addition of a synthetic gene.

- Athletes could use the same technique to enhance muscle size, strength, and resilience, and the treatment might be undetectable.

- When gene therapy enters the medical mainstream, preventing its abuse will be difficult, but attitudes toward genetic enhancement may also change.

seize any opportunity to gain an extra few split seconds of speed or a small boost in endurance.

Sports authorities fear that a new form of doping will be undetectable and thus much less preventable. Treatments that regenerate muscle, increase its strength, and protect it from degradation will soon be entering human clinical trials for muscle-wasting disorders. Among these are therapies that give patients a synthetic gene, which can last for years, producing high amounts of naturally occurring muscle-building chemicals.

This kind of gene therapy could transform the lives of the elderly and people with muscular dystrophy. Unfortunately, it is also a dream come true for an athlete bent on doping. The chemicals are indistinguishable from their natural counterparts and are only generated locally in the muscle tissue. Nothing enters the bloodstream, so officials will have nothing to detect in a blood or urine test. The World Anti-Doping Agency (WADA) has already asked scientists to help find ways to prevent gene therapy from becoming the newest means of doping. But as these treatments enter clinical trials and, eventually, widespread use, preventing athletes from gaining access to them could become impossible.

Is gene therapy going to form the basis of high-tech cheating in athletics? It is certainly possible. Will there be a time when gene therapy becomes so commonplace for disease that manipulating genes to enhance performance will become universally accepted? Perhaps. Either way, the world may be about to watch one of its last Olympic Games without genetically enhanced athletes.

Loss Leads to Gain

Research toward genetically enhancing muscle size and strength did not start out to serve the elite athlete. My own work began with observing members of my family, many of whom lived well into their 80s and 90s. Although they enjoyed generally good health, their quality of life suffered because of the weakness associated with aging. Both muscle strength and mass can decrease by as much as a third between the ages of 30 and 80.

There are actually three types of muscle in the body: smooth muscle, lining internal cavities such as the digestive tract; cardiac muscle in the heart; and skeletal muscle, the type most of us think of when we think of muscle. Skeletal muscle constitutes the largest organ of the body, and it is this type—particularly the strongest so-called fast fibers—that declines with age. With this loss of strength, losing one's balance is more likely and catching oneself before falling becomes more difficult. Once a fall causes a hip fracture or other serious injury, mobility is gone completely.

Skeletal muscle loss occurs with age in all mammals and probably results from a cumulative failure to repair damage caused by normal use. Intriguingly, aging-related changes in skeletal muscle resemble the functional and physical changes seen in a suite of diseases collectively known as muscular dystrophy, albeit at a much slower rate.

In the most common and most severe version of MD—Duchenne muscular dystrophy—an inherited gene mutation results in the absence of a protein called dystrophin that protects muscle fibers from injury by the force they exert during regular movement. Muscles are good at repairing themselves, although their normal regenerative mechanisms cannot keep up with the excessive rate of damage in MD. In aging muscles the rate of damage may be normal, but the repair mechanisms become less responsive. As a result, in both aging and Duchenne MD, muscle fibers die and are replaced by infiltrating fibrous tissue and fat.

In contrast, the severe skeletal muscle loss experienced by astronauts in microgravity and by patients immobilized by disability appears to be caused by a total shutdown of muscles' repair and growth mechanism at the same time apoptosis, or programmed cell death, speeds up. This phenomenon, known as disuse atrophy, is still not fully understood but makes sense from an evolutionary perspective. Skeletal muscle is metabolically expensive to maintain, so keeping a tight relation between muscle size and its activity saves energy. Skeletal muscle is exquisitely tuned to changing functional demands. Just as it withers with disuse, it grows in size, or hypertrophies, in response to repeated exertions. The increased load triggers a number of signaling pathways that lead to the addition of new cellular components within individual muscle fibers, changes in fiber type and, in extreme conditions, addition of new muscle fibers.

To be able to influence muscle growth, scientists are piecing together the molecular details of how muscle is naturally built and lost. Unlike the typical cell whose membrane contains liquid cytoplasm and a single nucleus, muscle cells are actually long cylinders, with multiple nuclei, and cytoplasm consisting of still more long tiny fibers called myofibrils. These myofibrils, in turn, are made of stacks of contractile units called sarcomeres. Collectively, their shortening produces muscle contractions, but the force they generate can damage the muscle fiber unless it is channeled outward. Dystrophin, the protein missing in Duchenne muscular dystrophy patients, conducts this energy across the muscle cell's membrane, protecting the fiber.

Yet even with dystrophin's buffering, muscle fibers are still injured by normal use. In fact, that is believed to be one way that exercise builds muscle mass and strength. Microscopic tears in the fibers caused by the exertion set off a chemical alarm that triggers tissue regeneration, which in muscle does not mean

The Body's Powerhouse

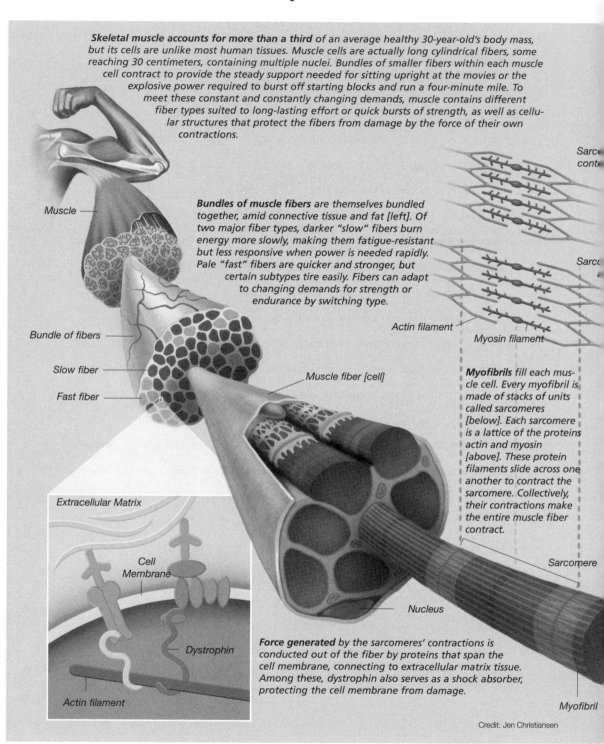

Skeletal muscle accounts for more than a third of an average healthy 30-year-old's body mass, but its cells are unlike most human tissues. Muscle cells are actually long cylindrical fibers, some reaching 30 centimeters, containing multiple nuclei. Bundles of smaller fibers within each muscle cell contract to provide the steady support needed for sitting upright at the movies or the explosive power required to burst off starting blocks and run a four-minute mile. To meet these constant and constantly changing demands, muscle contains different fiber types suited to long-lasting effort or quick bursts of strength, as well as cellular structures that protect the fibers from damage by the force of their own contractions.

Bundles of muscle fibers are themselves bundled together, amid connective tissue and fat [left]. Of two major fiber types, darker "slow" fibers burn energy more slowly, making them fatigue-resistant but less responsive when power is needed rapidly. Pale "fast" fibers are quicker and stronger, but certain subtypes tire easily. Fibers can adapt to changing demands for strength or endurance by switching type.

Myofibrils fill each muscle cell. Every myofibril is made of stacks of units called sarcomeres [below]. Each sarcomere is a lattice of the proteins actin and myosin [above]. These protein filaments slide across one another to contract the sarcomere. Collectively, their contractions make the entire muscle fiber contract.

Force generated by the sarcomeres' contractions is conducted out of the fiber by proteins that span the cell membrane, connecting to extracellular matrix tissue. Among these, dystrophin also serves as a shock absorber, protecting the cell membrane from damage.

Muscle

Bundle of fibers

Slow fiber

Fast fiber

Sarc
cont

Sarc
a

Actin filament

Myosin filament

Muscle fiber [cell]

Sarcomere

Nucleus

Myofibril

Extracellular Matrix

Cell
Membrane

Dystrophin

Actin filament

Credit: Jen Christiansen

production of new muscle fibers but rather repairing the outer membrane of existing fibers and plumping their interior with new myofibrils. Manufacturing this new protein requires activation of the relevant genes within the muscle cell's nuclei, and when the demand for myofibrils is great, additional nuclei are needed to bolster the muscle cell's manufacturing capacity.

Local satellite cells residing outside the muscle fibers answer this call. First these muscle-specific stem cells proliferate by normal cell division, then some of their progeny fuse with the muscle fiber, contributing their nuclei to the cell. Both progrowth and antigrowth factors are involved in regulating this process. Satellite cells respond to insulinlike growth factor I, or IGF-I, by undergoing a greater number of cell divisions, whereas a different growth-regulating factor, myostatin, inhibits their proliferation.

With these mechanisms in mind, about seven years ago my group at the University of Pennsylvania, in collaboration with Nadia Rosenthal and her colleagues at Harvard University, began to assess the possibility of using IGF-I to alter muscle function. We knew that if we injected the IGF-I protein alone, it would dissipate within hours. But once a gene enters a cell, it should keep functioning for the life of that cell, and muscle fibers are very long-lived. A single dose of the IGF-I gene in elderly humans would probably last for the rest of their lives. So we turned our attention to finding a way to deliver the IGF-I gene directly to muscle tissue.

Donning New Genes

Then as now, a major obstacle to successful gene therapy was the difficulty of getting a chosen gene into the desired tissue. Like many other researchers, we selected a virus as our delivery vehicle, or vector, because viruses are skilled at smuggling genes into cells. They survive and propagate by tricking the cells of a host organism into bringing the virus inside, rather like a biological Trojan horse. Once within the nucleus of a host cell, the virus uses the cellular machinery to replicate its genes and produce proteins. Gene therapists capitalize on this ability by loading a synthetic gene into the virus and removing any genes the virus could use to cause disease or to replicate itself. We selected a tiny virus called adeno-associated virus (AAV) as our vector, in part because it infects human muscle readily but does not cause any known disease.

We modified it with a synthetic gene that would produce IGF-I only in skeletal muscle and began by trying it out in normal mice. After injecting this AAV-IGF-I combination into young mice, we saw that the muscles' overall size and the rate at which they grew were 15 to 30 percent greater than normal, even though the mice were sedentary. Further, when we injected the gene into the muscles of middle-aged mice and then allowed them to reach old age, their muscles did not get any weaker.

To further evaluate this approach and its safety, Rosenthal created mice genetically engineered to overproduce IGF-I throughout their skeletal muscle. Encouragingly, they developed normally except for having skeletal muscles that ranged from 20 to 50 percent larger than those of regular mice. As these transgenic mice aged, their muscles retained a regenerative capacity typical of younger animals. Equally important, their IGF-I levels were elevated only in the muscles, not in the bloodstream, an important distinction because high circulating levels of IGF-I can cause cardiac problems and increase cancer risk. Subsequent experiments showed that IGF-I overproduction hastens muscle repair, even in mice with a severe form of muscular dystrophy.

Raising local IGF-I production allows us to achieve a central goal of gene therapy to combat muscle-wasting diseases: breaking the close connection between muscle use and its size. Simulating the results of muscle exercise in this manner also has obvious appeal to the elite athlete. Indeed, the rate of muscle growth in young sedentary animals suggested that this treatment could also be used to genetically enhance performance of healthy muscle. Recently my laboratory worked with an exercise physiology group headed by Roger P. Farrar of the University of Texas at Austin to test this theory.

We injected AAV-IGF-I into the muscle in just one leg of each of our lab rats and then subjected the animals to an eight-week weight-training protocol. At the end of the training, the AAV-IGF-I injected muscles had gained nearly twice as much strength as the uninjected legs in the same animals. After training stopped, the injected muscles lost strength much more slowly than the unenhanced muscle. Even in sedentary rats, AAV-IGF-I provided a 15 percent strength increase, similar to what we saw in the earlier mouse experiments.

We plan to continue our studies of IGF-I gene therapy in dogs because the golden retriever breed is susceptible to a particularly severe form of muscular dystrophy. We will also do parallel studies in healthy dogs to further test the effects and safety of inducing IGF-I overproduction. It is a potent growth and signaling factor, to which tumors also respond.

Safety concerns as well as unresolved questions about whether it is better to deliver AAV in humans through the bloodstream or by direct injection into muscle mean that approved gene therapy treatments using AAV-IGF-I could be as much as a decade away. In the shorter term, human trials of gene transfer to replace the dystrophin gene are already in planning stages, and the Muscular Dystrophy Association will soon begin a clinical trial of IGF-I injections to treat myotonic dystrophy, a condition that causes prolonged muscle contraction and, hence, damage.

A still more immediate approach to driving muscle hypertrophy may come from drugs designed to block myostatin. Precisely how myostatin inhibition builds muscle is still unclear, but myostatin seems to limit muscle growth throughout embryonic development and adult life. It acts as a brake on normal muscle growth and possibly as a promoter of atrophy when functional demands on muscle decrease. Experiments on genetically engineered mice indicate that the absence of this antigrowth factor results in considerably larger muscles because of both muscle fiber hypertrophy and hyperplasia, an excessive number of muscle fibers.

Making Muscle and More

Pharmaceutical and biotechnology companies are working on a variety of myostatin inhibitors. Initially, the possibility of producing meatier food animals piqued commercial interest. Nature has already provided examples of the effects of myostatin blockade in the Belgian Blue and Piedmontese cattle breeds, both of which have an inherited genetic mutation that produces a truncated, ineffective version of myostatin. These cattle are often called double-muscled, and their exaggerated musculature is all the more impressive because an absence of myostatin also interferes with fat deposition, giving the animals a lean, sculpted appearance.

The first myostatin-blocking drugs to have been developed are antibodies against myostatin, one of which may soon undergo clinical testing in muscular dystrophy patients. A different approach mimics the cattle mutation by creating a smaller version of myostatin, which lacks the normal molecule's signaling ability while retaining the structures that dock near satellite cells. This smaller protein, or peptide, essentially caps those docking locations, preventing myostatin from attaching to them. Injecting the peptide into mice produces skeletal muscle hypertrophy, and my colleagues and I will be attempting to create the same effect in our dog models by transferring a synthetic gene for the peptide.

Myostatin-blocking therapies also have obvious appeal to healthy people seeking rapid muscle growth. Although systemic drugs cannot target specific muscles, as gene transfer can, drugs have the benefit of easy delivery, and they can immediately be discontinued if a problem arises. On the other hand, such drugs would be relatively easy for sport regulatory agencies to detect with a blood test.

But what if athletes were to use a gene therapy approach similar to our AAV-IGF-I strategy? The product of the gene would be found just in the muscle, not in the blood or urine, and would be identical to its natural counterpart. Only a muscle biopsy could test for the presence of a particular synthetic gene or of a vector. But in the case of AAV, many people may be naturally infected with this harmless virus, so the test would not be conclusive for doping. Moreover, because most athletes would be unwilling to undergo an invasive biopsy before a competition, this type of genetic enhancement would remain virtually invisible.

And what of the safety of rapidly increasing muscle mass by 20 to 40 percent? Could an athlete sporting genetically inflated musculature exert enough force to snap his or her own bones or tendons? Probably not. We worry more about building muscle in elderly patients with bones weakened by osteoporosis. In a healthy young person, muscle growth occurring over weeks or months would give supporting skeletal elements time to grow to meet their new demands.

This safety question, however, is just one of the many that need further study in animals before these treatments can even be considered for mere enhancement of healthy humans. Nevertheless, with gene therapy poised to finally become a viable medical treatment, gene doping cannot be far behind, and overall muscle enlargement is but one way that it could be used. In sports such as sprinting, tweaking genes to convert muscle fibers to the fast type might also be desirable. For a marathoner, boosting endurance might be paramount.

Muscle is most likely to be the first tissue subject to genetic enhancement, but others could eventually follow. For example, endurance is also affected by

Natural Advantage

As this article went to press [2004], the *New England Journal of Medicine* was about to release the first documented description of a human being with a genetic mutation that wipes out myostatin production. Such cases have been discussed in scientific circles but never published because the subjects and their families usually do not wish to risk being identified. At least one of those families is rumored to include a European weight-lifting champion, which, if true, would not be surprising, given the tremendous advantage in muscle building and strength that a natural myostatin-suppressing mutation would confer.

But would it constitute an unfair advantage in an athlete, and would it justify other competitors using myostatin-inhibiting drugs or gene therapy simply to level the playing field? These questions are bound to be raised in continuing debate over the possibility of athletes using new muscle therapies to enhance their performance.

Natural "mutants" among athletes have been documented, among them an Olympic gold medalist. Finnish cross-country skier Eero Mäntyranta won two gold medals in the 1964 Winter Olympics. But it was not until decades later that Finnish scientists identified a genetic mutation in Mäntyranta's entire family that causes an excessive response to erythropoietin, leading to extraordinarily high numbers of oxygen-carrying red blood cells. Several of his family members, it the amount of oxygen reaching muscles. Erythropoietin is a naturally occurring protein that spurs development of oxygen-carrying red blood cells. Its synthetic form, a drug called Epoietin, or simply EPO, was developed to treat anemia but has been widely abused by athletes—most publicly by cyclists in the 1998 Tour de France. An entire team was excluded from that race when their EPO use was uncovered, yet EPO abuse in sports continues.

turns out, were also champion endurance athletes.

In addition to mutations with dramatic effects, investigators have also begun to discover natural gene variants that more subtly favor certain kinds of athletic activity. For example, last year Australian researchers examined a gene called *ACTN3* in a group of male and female elite sprinters. Nearly 20 percent of people lack a functional version of this gene that gives rise to a protein specific to fast muscle fibers, although a less effective protein normally compensates for its absence. The scientists found an unusually high frequency of the working *ACTN3* gene in the sprinters, however. In particular, more of the female sprinters had two copies of the gene than would be expected in a randomly selected group.

Many research groups are trying to identify other gene variants that give athletes an edge by maximizing oxygen uptake, heart efficiency, power output, endurance or other traits. More than 90 genes or chromosomal locations have been associated with athletic performance so far, and this research is already provoking its own ethical controversies. Critics fear that based on their genetic makeup, children will be recruited into certain sports or, if they lack the right gene mix, denied a chance to advance to the elite level of sports training. Even selective breeding for superathletes has been predicted.

A more certain result of scanning athletes' genomes will be the discovery that some of them, like Mäntyranta's, contain true genetic mutations that amount to genetic enhancement. Such revelations will add still more complexity to ethical arguments over the prospect of gene doping in sports.

Pumping Up with Genes

Building athletes' muscle, tweaking its composition, and boosting endurance are enhancements theoretically possible with gene therapy. Using a synthetic gene to simulate an injury signal spurs repair activity by stem cells [right], leaving muscle fibers bigger and stronger. Activating a dormant gene or adding a new one could change muscle fiber types [below]. Unlike systemic drugs, gene therapy also allows key muscle subgroups to be targeted based on the biomechanics of a given sport.

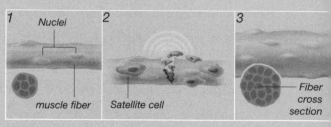

1 Nuclei
muscle fiber
2 Satellite cell
3 Fiber cross section

In normal muscle, a fiber's multiple nuclei [1] are responsible for driving the manufacture of new proteins. When repair is needed, chemical signals from the wound draw satellite cells, which proliferate before fusing with the fiber to contribute their nuclei to the effort [2]. The addition of more nuclei and fresh myofibrils leaves a repaired fiber bulkier than before it was injured [3].

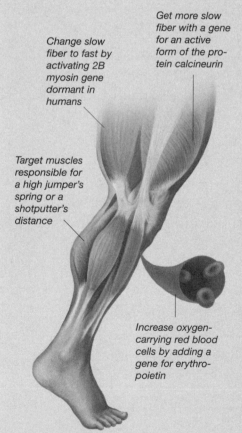

Change slow fiber to fast by activating 2B myosin gene dormant in humans

Get more slow fiber with a gene for an active form of the protein calcineurin

Target muscles responsible for a high jumper's spring or a shotputter's distance

Increase oxygen-carrying red blood cells by adding a gene for erythropoietin

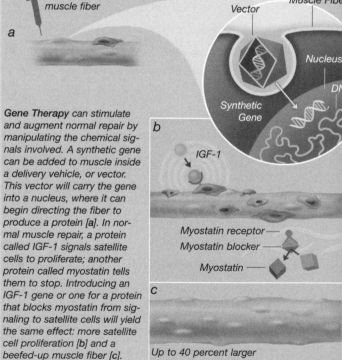

a Injection of gene into muscle fiber

Vector
Muscle Fiber
Synthetic Gene
Nucleus
DN

b IGF-1
Myostatin receptor
Myostatin blocker
Myostatin

c Up to 40 percent larger

Gene Therapy can stimulate and augment normal repair by manipulating the chemical signals involved. A synthetic gene can be added to muscle inside a delivery vehicle, or vector. This vector will carry the gene into a nucleus, where it can begin directing the fiber to produce a protein [a]. In normal muscle repair, a protein called IGF-1 signals satellite cells to proliferate; another protein called myostatin tells them to stop. Introducing an IGF-1 gene or one for a protein that blocks myostatin from signaling to satellite cells will yield the same effect: more satellite cell proliferation [b] and a beefed-up muscle fiber [c].

Credit: Jen Cristiansen

Gene transfer to raise erythropoietin production has already been tried in animals, with results that illustrate the potential dangers of prematurely attempting such enhancements in humans. In 1997 and 1998 scientists tried transferring synthetic erythropoietin genes into monkeys and baboons. In both experiments, the animals' red blood cell counts nearly doubled within 10 weeks, producing blood so thick that it had to be regularly diluted to keep their hearts from failing.

The technology necessary to abuse gene transfer is certainly not yet within reach of the average athlete. Still, officials in the athletic community fear that just as technically skilled individuals have turned to the manufacture and sale of so-called designer steroids, someday soon a market in genetic enhancement may emerge. Policing such abuse will be much harder than monitoring drug use, because detection will be difficult.

It is also likely, however, that in the decades to come, some of these gene therapies will be proved safe and will become available to the general population. If the time does arrive when genetic enhancement is widely used to improve quality of life, society's ethical stance on manipulating our genes will probably be much different than it is today. Sports authorities already acknowledge that muscle-regenerating therapies may be useful in helping athletes to recover from injuries.

So will we one day be engineering superathletes or simply bettering the health of the entire population with gene transfer? Even in its infancy, this technology clearly has tremendous potential to change both sports and our society. The ethical issues surrounding genetic enhancement are many and complex. But for once, we have time to discuss and debate them before the ability to use this power is upon us.

Scientific American, July 2004

Doping by Design

Why new steroids are easy to make and hard to detect

STEVEN ASHLEY

A furor erupted in the world of sports last fall when chemists announced that they had identified a new performance-enhancing synthetic steroid undetectable by standard antidoping tests. Scientists familiar with androgenic steroids and their illicit use in athletics were not at all surprised. "We've known about designer steroids for many years, but up to now we've never been able to prove that someone is actually making them," says Don H. Catlin, a molecular pharmacologist and director of the Olympic Analytical Laboratory at the University of California at Los Angeles. Catlin led the effort to isolate and analyze tetrahydrogestrinone (THG), the compound at the center of the storm. "The fact that we finally characterized one is certainly no reason to celebrate. I'm much more worried about the next THG out there that we haven't found yet."

That's because it is fairly easy for organic chemists to design novel anabolic steroids that standard drug tests would not detect. (Identification depends on knowing the compound's structure beforehand; THG use was discovered only because an anonymous coach sent a spent syringe to U.S. antidoping officials.) All androgenic steroids are based on a chemical structure featuring a central complex of four hexagonal carbon rings. Small changes to the molecular groups attached to the periphery of central ring complex yield new derivatives. "Nature has made thousands of steroids, and chemists can make thousands more relatively easily," Catlin comments.

Bulk Up, Get Sick

Synthetic anabolic steroids build muscle mass and endurance as well as permit faster recovery after strenuous activity, but proving those effects scientifically has been surprisingly difficult. First, athletes get a major placebo effect from doping themselves. Second, the dosages they typically use are many times as high as the levels that human-experimentation committees would approve. Focusing on the obvious benefits, users fail to recognize steroids' toxic side effects, some of which take time to manifest themselves: severe acne, heart disease, liver damage and uncontrollable rage.

Rogue scientists start with testosterone or its commercially available analogues and then make minor structural modifications to yield similarly active derivatives. The underground chemists make no effort to test their creations for effectiveness or safety, of course. Production of a simple new steroid compound would require "lab equipment costing maybe $50,000 to $100,000," Catlin estimates. Depending on the number of chemical reactions needed for synthesis, "some of them could be made in a week or two. Others might take six months to a year."

"There are lots of good steroid chemists offshore who gained their expertise developing contraceptives and other hormone drugs decades ago," says Jean D. Wilson, an expert in androgen physiology at the University of Texas Southwestern Medical Center at Dallas. Now that birth-control pills have become a commodity product, "many of these experienced organic chemists are sitting around twiddling their thumbs," he says. "There must be thousands of people in the world who could readily synthesize designer steroids." The THG episode fuels speculation that a network of clandestine laboratories exists that develops and produces illegal steroids.

THG's chemical structure is similar to that of trenbolone and gestrinone, both synthetic anabolic steroids banned for athletic use by international sports federations. "Trenbolone is a veterinary drug used by cattle ranchers to increase the size of their stock," Wilson says. It is also popular with body-builders, despite toxic side effects. The structure of gestrinone, used to treat endometriosis and related illnesses, differs from that of THG by only four hydrogen atoms. In fact, once Catlin and his U.C.L.A. colleagues had deduced the structure of THG, they re-created it by hydrogenating (adding hydrogen atoms to) gestrinone, which yielded tetrahydrogestrinone.

Besides its novelty, a synthetic steroid's chemical stability under testing conditions also affects its chances of detection. THG tends to break down when prepared for analysis by standard means, which helps to explain why Catlin's team did not identify the compound in its first attempt. The U.C.L.A. chemists isolated THG's signature only after switching to a more sensitive assay process. They used liquid and gas chromatography to fraction-ate the sample into its molecular constituents; an electron beam then frag-mented the separated molecules in a mass spectrometer to produce a spectrum indicating the basic chemical components. The group subsequently developed a urine test for THG, which has been used to finger several well-known sports figures.

Still, the cat-and-mouse game that is athletic drug testing continues. The trouble is that the mice are fast-moving targets that never stop evolving. "We're looking forward for our next research project, and that includes look-ing for other designer steroids," Catlin reports. Perhaps they can pounce before the mouse disappears.

Scientific American, February 2004

Catchy Carbon

*What Floyd Landis has in common
with ocean sediment*

SARAH SIMPSON

When marine chemist John Hayes pioneered a way to scrutinize the carbon atoms in seafloor mud 15 years ago, he was trying to unravel mysteries about how dead microbes once lived. Never did he guess that sporting officials would one day use his invention to catch drug cheats.

By modifying Hayes's method to examine the carbon atoms in athletes' urine, medical researchers at the U.C.L.A. Olympic Laboratory have developed the first definitive screen for synthetic testosterone, a popular anabolic steroid banned by most sports organizations since the 1970s. The new test—known as the carbon isotope ratio (CIR) test—figures prominently in several recent, high-profile doping cases, including the disqualification of sprinter Justin Gatlin's world record in the 100 meters. It may also strip cyclist Floyd Landis of his 2006 Tour de France title.

Before the CIR test became standard protocol in the late 1990s, analysts relied on a more primitive urine screen that could recognize only higher-than-average ratios of testosterone to a related compound known as epitestosterone. But because these so-called T/E ratios are naturally elevated in some people, accusing an athlete of doping required follow-up exams, U.C.L.A. lab director Don H. Catlin explains. If subsequent urine samples contained lower T/E ratios, officials assumed a synthetic substance caused the initial spike. But if later screens matched the preliminary results, officials had to declare the athlete drug-free—even though a person could beat the test by ingesting artificial testosterone throughout the testing period, Catlin says.

What sport needed was a way to differentiate testosterone made in a factory from that produced in the body. Catlin and his colleagues knew they needed to find a distinct chemical fingerprint in the hormone that would allow them to trace the carbon atoms to one source or the other—just the way Hayes was able to determine whether his dead microbes ate the carbon dioxide in seawater or the methane bubbling up through gooey seafloor sediment.

As standard practice, pharmaceutical companies build testosterone molecules from a framework of carbon atoms derived from wild yams or soybeans. These warm-climate plants and their kin process carbon differently than do the more abundant, temperate-climate plants such as corn. This processing leaves the soy relatives notably depleted in carbon 13, an isotope that has one extra neutron and thus a slightly greater mass than the common isotope, carbon 12.

If the testosterone in an athlete's urine carries the soylike fingerprint, as Gatlin's and Landis's did, it sticks out like a sore thumb when compared with cholesterol or other hormones in the same urine sample. Those reference hormones, like all compounds produced by the human body, contain more carbon 13 (relative to carbon 12) than soy does. The variety of plant material in the food we eat—everything from apples to zucchini and even to the corn a feedlot cow consumes before becoming a hamburger—gives the naturally produced hormones their diagnostic enrichment.

The CIR test "strikes me as pretty close to bulletproof," says Hayes, now at the Woods Hole Oceanographic Institution. Changing the carbon isotope fingerprint of naturally secreted testosterone without also changing that of the reference hormones would be nearly impossible, he explains. Dehydration, alcohol consumption and many of the other excuses bandied about by accused athletes would simply have no effect. Only if the body were able to make testosterone from an artificial compound—such as the cortisone athletes sometimes inject to reduce muscle inflammation—might the natural hormone carry a synthetic-looking fingerprint, Hayes notes.

Catlin predicts that the efficacy of the CIR test, which also identifies a range of compounds related to testosterone, will make athletes think twice before taking steroids—unless dopers find a new way to beat the system. Until then, it seems they should heed an old adage: you are what you eat.

Scientific American, November 2006

THE ATHLETE'S MIND

Psyched Up, Psyched Out

Some athletes swear by it. Others laugh at it. Can science determine if sports psychology works?

MICHAEL SHERMER

Although I was trained as an experimental psychologist, I didn't become interested in how psychology could enhance athletic performance until 1981. That's when I began preparing to compete in the first annual 3,000-mile, nonstop transcontinental bicycle race, the Race Across America. I thought I had better try any technique I could find to prepare my mind for the pain and pressures of what *Outside* magazine calls "the world's toughest race."

In addition to riding 500 miles a week and subjecting my body to such "treatments" as chiropractic, Rolfing, mud baths, megavitamins, iridology and electrical stimulation, I listened to motivational tapes. I meditated. I chanted. I attended seminars by Jack Schwarz, an Oregon-based healing guru who taught us "voluntary controls of internal states." I contacted Gina Kuras, a hypnotherapist who taught me self-hypnosis to control pain, overcome motivational lows, maintain psychological highs and stay focused. I got so good at going deep into a hypnotic trance that when ABC's *Wide World of Sports* came to my home to film a session, Gina could not immediately bring me back, causing her to fear that I had somehow harmed myself.

Did all this New Age fiddle-faddle work? I really can't say it did, as a scientist or a cyclist. Still, I'm glad I had these crutches during my 10 days of leg-burning, lung-searing riding. As Mark Victor Hansen, an apostle of the motivation movement and co-author of the *Chicken Soup for the Soul* book series, would chant, "This stuff works when you work it."

On one level Hansen is right. As with fad diets, it matters less which one you are on and more that you are doing something—anything—about your eating habits. Diets are really a form of behavioral, not caloric, modification. The point is to be vigilant and focused, thinking about the problem and trying different solutions.

But the deeper and more important question is: Can we say scientifically that sports psychology techniques work? Obtaining an answer is complicated, because so many of these self-help methods are based on anecdotal evidence. As my social science colleague, Frank Sulloway, likes to point out: "Anecdotes do not make a science. Ten anecdotes are no better than one, and 100 anecdotes are no better than 10."

Without controlled comparison groups, there is no way to know if an effect that was observed was the result of chance or the technique. Did you win the race because of the meditation or because you had a deep sleep, a good meal, new equipment or made progress in your training? Even if a dozen athletes who applied a certain procedure before an event performed better, without a control group there is no way to know what really led to the improvement. And when we say that an athlete performed "better"—better than what? Better than ever? Better than yesterday? Better than average? Conducting a scientific evaluation of the effectiveness of psychological aids on athletic performance is a messy business.

The Desire to Win

Sports psychology began in the 1890s, when Indiana University psychologist Norman Triplett, an avid cyclist, performed a series of studies to determine why cyclists ride faster in groups than when they are alone. Triplett discovered that the presence of others, whether competitors or spectators, motivates athletes to greater performance. As sports have become professionalized, the field has paralleled the trends in general psychology, applying behavioral models (how rewards and punishment shape performance), psycho-physiological models (the relation between heart rate and brain-wave activity and performance) and cognitive-behavioral models (the connection between self-confidence and anxiety with performance).

The goal, of course, is to understand, predict, and enhance the thinking and behavior of athletes. Studies show that a cyclist will ride faster when another cyclist is riding alongside or even behind than when the cyclist is alone. And the average cyclist will race faster against a competitor than against the clock. Why? One reason is "social facilitation," a theory in which individual behavior is shaped by the presence and motivation of a group (think mass rallies and rock concerts). But what is actually going on inside the athlete's brain and body? Well, competition provides the promise of positive (and the threat of negative) reinforcement, stimulates an increase in physiological activity and arousal, and locks the athlete into a self-generating feedback loop between performance expectations and outcomes. This constant feedback causes competitors to push one another to the limits of their physical capabilities.

Mr. Clutch vs. Mr. Choke

Yet as in all psychological situations, outside variables alter the theoretical effect. Competition and crowds can increase an athlete's anxiety, causing him or her to crumble under fans' expectations. Basketballs that swish in during practice clank off the rim in the game; aces on the practice court turn into double faults at center court. But the same stimulation can accelerate the heart rate and adrenaline of another athlete, accentuating the drive to win. Some athletes are at ease under pressure: Reggie Jackson as "Mr. October," Jerry West as "Mr. Clutch." Others falter: Bill Buckner's infamous through-the-legs error at first base that cost the Boston Red Sox the crucial Game 6 of the 1986 World Series; Scott Norwood's muffed field goal in the closing seconds of the Buffalo Bills's best opportunity for a Super Bowl ring thus far.

Sports psychologists offer several explanations for this variance. It comes down to personality: some individuals are just better at risk taking, competitiveness, self-confidence, expectation for success and the ability to regulate stress. And some have an easier time hewing to the basic winning habits of professional athletes: practice a lot, come prepared with a contingency plan for changes in the competition, stay focused on the event and block out distracting stimuli, follow one's own plan and not those of the competitor, don't get flustered by unexpected events, learn from mistakes, and never give up.

The complexity of the task and the nature of the competitive situation also affect each athlete's ability to rise or fall in the heat of competition. The 100,000 screaming fans lining the final kilometers of a crippling climb up the

French Alps in the Tour de France might catapult a cyclist onto the winner's podium but could cause a golfer to knock his five-foot putt into the sand trap or a gymnast to do a face plant into the mat. Context counts.

So does attitude. Psyching out an opponent is another mental game that can affect an athlete's performance. It is extremely complicated to test; suffice it to say that it can happen. And place a vote for Muhammad Ali as the greatest practitioner in history. Ali imposed his own psychological edge over rivals better than any athlete in the 20th century, earning him the title of "The Greatest."

Home-Court Advantage

Physiological arousal also tampers with an athlete's performance; too little or too much are both deleterious. And, again, each athlete varies in how much arousal is ideal for peak performance. Russian sports psychologist Yuri Hanin, for example, describes "zones of optimal functioning," in which athlete A does best when minimally aroused, athlete B performs best at a medium level of arousal, and athlete C responds to a high level of arousal.

Arousal of an entire team may explain, or debunk, the so-called home-court advantage. We all "know" that competitors have an advantage when playing at home. Teams strive all season to finish with the best record in order to get it. Research shows that on average and in the long run, football and baseball teams do slightly better at their own stadiums than at their competitors', and basketball and hockey teams do significantly better at home than away (the smaller arenas presumably enhance social facilitation). But the advantage may hold only for regular-season games. The influence seems to wane during preseason and postseason play. For example, a study of World Series contests from 1924 to 1982 showed that in series that went five games or more, the home team won 60 percent of the first two games but only 40 percent of the remaining games. Interestingly, in the 26 series that went to a nail-biting seventh game, the home team came away empty-handed 62 percent of the time.

Since 1983, however, the trend has shifted somewhat. In analyzing the data, I found that between 1983 and 1999 the home team won only 54 percent of the first two games but went on to win 80 percent of the deciding seventh games. Perhaps teams, like individual players, vary in their zones of optimal functioning. It is also possible that in some instances overzealous fans become fanatics (whence the term comes) in the final stretch, driving their teams into such an intense state of unrealistic expectations that it stymies performance. Or helps it.

What the ambiguous outcome of this scientific analysis tells us is that human variation confounds the predictive validity of most sports psychology models. As all evolutionary biologists know—and experimental psychologists tend to forget—variation within a species is the norm, not the exception. And in few species is variation more pronounced in so many variables than in humans. Throw into this mix the complications of social and cultural sports factors, and the models break down.

The Lie of Being "In the Groove"

Science has also shed light on the psychological notion of peak performance. It is one of those fuzzy concepts athletes talk about in equally fuzzy expressions, such as being "in sync," "in the groove," "in the zone," "letting go" and "playing in a trance." Psychologists describe it with such adjectives as "relaxed," "focused," "energized," "absorbed" and "controlled." But these are just ways to describe some poorly understood connection between mental states and physical performance. Something—we don't know what—is going on inside the brain and body that allows the athlete, every once in a while, to put it all together. The golf ball drops into the cup instead of skirting the edge. The hit baseball always falls where they ain't. The basketballs swish in one after another. When you're hot, you're hot.

But maybe not. Streaks in sports can be tested by statisticians who specialize in probabilities. Intuitively we believe that hot streaks are real, and everyone from casino operators to sports bookies counts on us to act on this belief. But in a fascinating 1985 study of "hot hands" in basketball, Stanford University behavioral scientist Amos Tversky and his colleagues analyzed every shot taken by the Philadelphia 76ers for an entire season. They discovered that the probability of a player hitting a second shot did not increase following an initial successful basket beyond what would be expected by chance and the average shooting percentage of the player.

In fact, what they found is so counterintuitive that it is jarring: the number of streaks (successful baskets in sequence) did not exceed the predictions of a statistical coin-flip model. If you conduct a coin-flip experiment and record heads or tails, you will shortly encounter streaks. On average and in the long run, you will flip five heads or tails in a row once in every 32 sequences of five tosses. Because Tversky was dealing with professional basketball players, however, adjustments in the formula were made to account for ability. If a player's shooting percentage is 60 percent, for example, chance dictates that he will sink six baskets in a row once in every 20 sequences of six shots attempted. When average shooting percentage was controlled for, Tversky found that there were no shooting sequences beyond what was indicated by chance. Players might feel "hot" or "in flow" when they have games that fall into the high range of chance, but science shows that nothing happens beyond what probability says should happen.

How to Avoid Choking

Even Michael Jordan makes mistakes. No matter how good an athlete is, "choking" is inevitable. The difference is that the pros have trained both mentally and physically to reduce its likelihood and to recover from it. Sports psychologists Robin Vealey of Miami University of Ohio and Daniel Gould of the University of North Carolina at Greensboro offer some tips:

Focus. Choking often occurs when your thoughts are on the past or the future. Focus on the present, and be conscious of your emotional and physical reactions to a stressful situation.

Practice. Practice in stressful situations in order to get used to physical and mental tension. Mental and muscle memory interact, and you can train them together to create conditioned responses to tense circumstances.

Relax. Stress makes your mind hurry and your muscles tense up. Use breathing techniques to relax, and consciously loosen tight muscle groups.

Talk to yourself. Self-talk can calm, remotivate and remind you of your best technique. Use a "mantra with meaning"—for example, a tennis player can remind herself to have "quick feet" so she is moving and ready. And don't obsess over a mistake; instead replace a negative mental image of yourself with a positive one to bring you back into the game.

Know yourself and your environment. Perceived pressure from teammates, coaches and yourself can cause you to freeze up. Remember: it's just a game. Pick the challenges and competitions you think you can handle.

—Naomi Lubick

There is one exception to this principle: occasionally, all the human variables can come together in a unique fashion that leads to a performance so rare that it is not matched for decades, or ever. Bob Beamon's unbelievable long jump of 29 feet, 2.5 inches, at the 1968 Olympic Games in Mexico City, surpassed the old mark by a remarkable 21.75 inches and was not bettered for more than two decades. Even more remarkable was Joe DiMaggio's 56-game hitting streak. It was a feat so many standard deviations away from the mean that, in the words of physicist Ed Purcell and paleontologist Stephen Jay Gould, who calculated its probability, it "should not have happened at all." It ranks as perhaps the greatest achievement in modern sports. Individual greatness can defy science and throws a new wrench into the tightly coiled machinery of psychological theory.

Does Visualization Work?

Like most social scientists, sports psychologists are much better at understanding behavior than at predicting or controlling it. It is one thing to model all the variables that cause some athletes to triumph and others to flounder. It is harder to predict which athletes will step up to the winner's podium and virtually impossible to turn Andy Airball into Michael Jordan. Here we enter the murky world of performance enhancement and sports counseling—the art of sports psychology.

One of the most common and effective techniques is imagery training, or visualization, wherein an athlete envisions himself executing the physical sequences of the sport. We have all seen Olympic downhill skiers minutes before their run standing in place with their eyes closed, their bodies gyrating through the course. Gymnasts and ice skaters are also big on visualization. Even cyclists practice it: Lance Armstrong attributed his extraordinary 1999 Tour de France victory in part to the fact that he rode every stage of the race ahead of time, so that during the race itself he could imagine what was coming and execute his preplanned attacks. Countless experiments show that groups that receive physical and imagery training on a novel task do better than groups that receive only physical training.

Nevertheless, failures of imagery-trained athletes are legion. We hear about Lance Armstrong but not about all those other cyclists who mentally rode the Tour ahead of time and finished in the middle of the pack. We don't hear about the visualizing downhill skiers who crash or the imagining gymnasts who flop. Did riding the course ahead of time give Armstrong a psychological edge or just a better race plan? Visualization may be little more than good, utilitarian planning.

Even the most enthusiastic supporters of imagery training caution that numerous variables can interfere with the technique's benefits. University of North Carolina sports psychologists Daniel Gould and Nicole Damarjian caution that "imagery is like any physical skill. It requires systematic practice to develop and refine. Individual athletes will differ in their ability to image. Imagery is not a magical cure for performance woes."

Flooded with Flapdoodle

What Gould and Damarjian seem to be saying is that this stuff works when you work it. But what does that mean? To determine if a psychological technique "works," we might evaluate it by two standards: whether it works for an individual and whether it works for everyone. For the athlete who wins the gold medal, whatever he or she did "worked." It does not matter what scientists think of the techniques that were used, because there was a positive outcome. That satisfies the first criterion.

But will a given technique used by that winning athlete work for all athletes? Here we face a problem that hangs like an albatross around the neck of clinical psychology. There is very little experimental evidence to suggest that it will. I do not go as far as psychiatrist Thomas Szasz in his claim that mental illnesses are all socially constructed. Nor do I accept all of clinical psychologist Tana Dineen's argument that the "psychology industry" is "manufacturing victims" in order to feed its growing economic juggernaut. But these two extremists have injected a badly needed dose of skepticism into a field flooded with flapdoodle. Both the practitioners and participants in sports psychology would be well advised to step back and ask themselves whether it is good enough if an individual believes a technique helps and, if not, how science can prove it has value.

So did all the psychological exercises I tried "work" for me in the Race Across America? It is impossible to say, because I was a subject pool of one and there were no controls. When I wanted them to work, it seemed like they did, and maybe that's good enough. Yet I cannot help but wonder if a few more hours in the training saddle every day might have made a bigger difference. Sports can be psychological, but they are first and foremost physical. Although body and mind are integrated, I would caution not to put mind above body.

Scientific American Presents: Building the Elite Athlete, Fall 2000

The Will to Win

*More and more athletes are engaging in mental
workouts to give them that extra edge*

STEVE J. AYAN

The Olympic stadium was silent. The spectators held their collective breath.
The 100-meter finalists, crouched against their starting blocks, raised their
backs as the starter raised his pistol and announced, "Set . . . !" Each powerful sprinter, poised to explode when the gun went off, was keenly aware of
what hung in the balance. They had trained to exhaustion every day for years
to prepare their bodies for this one race.

But had they disciplined their minds? The runner who would break the
tape would need more than strong muscles, heart and lungs. He would need
concentration, control, confidence—and an unerring eye on the finish line.
At this tense moment, one mistimed twitch could cause a false start and cost
him the race. But if he eased off in any way, his first steps would lag behind
those of his competitors, guaranteeing a loss. "Bang!"

Sports psychology is a booming business. Part of the reason is because
elite athletes in many sports are getting closer and closer to one another in
terms of physical prowess and talents, leaving thoughts and feelings as the x-
factor that brings victory. Many top athletes now find mental training indis-
pensable—and not just for performing on race or game day but for getting
the most out of daily workouts. Many seek help from psychologists, but others go elsewhere: Tour de France champion Lance Armstrong receives regular
psychological exercises as well as a daily physical training plan from his per-

sonal coach, Chris Carmichael. Formula One auto-racing ace Michael Schumacher has a personal cook, Balbir Singh, who is rumored to double as his spiritual adviser. Others simply rely on personal rituals to focus their tennis serve or home-run swing.

Often there is little scientific basis for athletes' mental gymnastics, and the placebo effect cannot be completely ruled out, yet the practices seem to provide a tailwind. Studies show that athletes may profit most by building up psychological strength through three techniques: visualization, confidence and self-talk. The same exercises can work for recreational athletes, too.

See It

Although sports psychologists have supported athletes for more than 30 years, the profession was largely informal until 1983, when the U.S. Olympic Committee established a sports psychology registry. In 1986 the Association for the Advancement of Applied Sport Psychology was founded to promote related science and practices. Since then, the profession has grown briskly: for its 2004 conference, the association received 450 potential presentations.

The practice of visualizing an athletic movement in order to perfect it became popular in the 1970s. Tennis players were among the early adopters. A player standing quietly on the court with his eyes closed would imagine himself hitting the ball, thinking to himself something like: "My racket is an extension of my arm. My entire body is tingling with excitement, but I am utterly relaxed. I am enjoying every ball that comes flying toward me. I am absolutely sure that with my next stroke I can place the ball in any corner of my opponent's court. The court is enormously wide." Psychologist Mihaly Csikszentmihalyi, now at Claremont Graduate University, coined the term "flow" in 1975 to describe this kind of feeling: complete confidence in one's own actions, blocking out distractions, reveling in the experience.

To put herself into such an ideal performance state, an athlete seeks a healthy balance of strain and relaxation. She must become completely immersed in her own movements. A high jumper must see in her mind exactly each step of her run-up and takeoff and then watch her body glide over the bar. In most visualization training, this focus is achieved by learning to see and subsequently control each concrete component of a movement. In tennis, for example, each stroke consists of "swing, hit, follow-through." With practice, a tennis player can see the ideal motion with the mind's eye.

Visualization can benefit training, too, by helping to transform complex motor procedures into automatic movements. The effects on the body of visualization were demonstrated more than a century ago. In the late 1800s English physiologist William Carpenter discovered that imagining movements could elicit reactions in muscles. When we see a soccer player strike a ball toward the goal, our own leg muscles may contract, imperceptibly if not noticeably. This "ideomotor" (or Carpenter) effect, with repeated visualization, can make the real motion easier to perform.

More recently, brain researchers have studied this phenomenon with imaging technologies. Stephen M. Kosslyn, a psychologist at Harvard University, discovered that imagining a movement activates the same motor regions of the cerebral cortex that light up during the actual movement. Most researchers theorize that repeatedly visualizing the movement strengthens or adds synaptic connections among relevant neurons. Some basketball players and coaches, for example, claim that repeatedly visualizing the ideal arm and hand motions for a free throw from the foul line improves players' success rates in actual games: bend the knees, flex the elbow, cock the wrist, then let the ball roll off the fingertips.

And yet some studies indicate that breaking a motion down into parts and concentrating on them in succession can hinder fluid coordination. The alternative is to imagine the outcome—not the motion but its result, such as the ball dropping through the net. Golfer Tiger Woods reports that it is easier for him to sink putts when he imagines the rattle of the ball in the cup.

Believe It

Automating one's movements frees up the brain to concentrate on other aspects of an athletic challenge. But even more mind control is needed. Witness the so-called training champions, who perform outstandingly in workouts but falter or choke when the pressure is on during a real race or game. This perplexing situation is familiar to anyone who has smoothly practiced a joke or magic trick over and over but then stumbles when performing it before an audience. It can be difficult for an athlete facing high stakes, championships and sold-out stadiums to keep calm.

Confidence is the antidote, and it comes from a combination of courage, tolerance and attitude. The success of Ukrainian pole-vaulter Sergei Bubka, who won six world championships in the 1980s and 1990s, showed just how important courage can be. Bubka did not dominate his event because of extraordinary physical talent. In this physically and technically demanding sport, every vaulter's knees tremble just before he starts his approach to the bar. But not Bubka's. After hoisting his pole, he would run toward the pit like a crazy man, as if he had no fear at all.

Most champion athletes are usually in good psychological shape; if they weren't, they would not have reached such a high level of achievement. Various studies have found that top athletes have a greater ability to concentrate and a stronger will to perform than ordinary mortals. These athletes brim with self-confidence during competitions. Part of this surety is an attitude that is purposely exuded to intimidate competitors. Mostly, however, confidence stems from an athlete's faith in himself. That faith is built by regularly setting high but achievable goals in training and in competition. Attaining these goals and then subsequent ones builds motivation and leads to volition—imagining and achieving any goal desired. With full confidence, individuals can overcome enormous challenges.

For endurance athletes, a large part of their confidence comes from knowing how to tolerate pain, how to push their bodies right up to the pain barrier—and then go beyond it. When the 2004 Tour de France races reached the critical point where the leaders would finally break away from the head pack, Jan Ullrich's German teammate Udo Bolts would yell at him: "Torture yourself, you bastard!"

Professional as well as weekend athletes can develop the ability to shut out pain or fear by training hard. They must also expose themselves to the extreme demands of an actual event repeatedly until the ability to tolerate the intensity becomes routine. Furthermore, to rebound from the physical and psychic stress that these experiences impose, muscular and mental relaxation techniques may be in order. One way to reduce anxiety is autogenic training, which teaches athletes to repeat autosuggestive formulas such as "I am completely calm." Physical relief can come from practices such as progressive muscle relaxation, which involves alternating contractions and relaxations of individual body parts—say, a thigh or shoulder.

Learning to deal with stress and strain is a cornerstone of mental training—one that ideally begins well before a crisis. The possible consequences of constant pressure to perform—experienced today by almost every top athlete—are readily apparent. Fear of failure, inadequate recovery time and unending media harassment are fatiguing, especially for younger, less experienced competitors. When it appears these athletes are at the breaking point, that of course is usually when coaches call in a psychologist. But often it is too late. Many coaches call for expert help only when a situation is already critical. Studies indicate that more than two thirds of all interventions by sports psychologists are done during times of acute problems and crises. Instead of putting out fires, coaches should consider ongoing care, so mental problems can be caught and treated early, before performance suffers.

Say It

Nevertheless, some anxiety is unavoidable, and that may not be bad. Coaches often tell their players that a little nervousness is good because it keeps them on their toes. Too much anxiety limits performance, however. Self-talk is a leading method for reducing doubt and anxiety. Boxer Muhammad Ali, who strutted around before every match loudly proclaiming, "I am the greatest!" is probably the most famous practitioner of this technique. Such directed speaking increases one's will to endure.

The value of self-talk was demonstrated in a classic 1977 sports psychology study. Michael Mahoney, then at Pennsylvania State University, working with coach Marshall Avener, asked a group of gymnasts what they thought about and what they said to themselves during competitions. It turned out that the most successful athletes—those who qualified for the Olympic team—were no less plagued by doubt and anxiety than their less successful colleagues. But they compensated better by constantly encouraging themselves, more so than those who finished with lower scores.

The need for self-encouragement is highest in sports where winning is determined by subjective judges, such as gymnastics or figure skating. There is no clear order of finish like that in a 100-meter dash or a cycling race. Success in team sports is measured by "softer" criteria, too. Individuals can play well, and the team can still lose. The team needs a strong sense of collective identity. A soccer team, for example, must consist not of 11 individuals but of 11 friends.

A recreational athlete can exploit the same mental tricks that the pros use, whether it is talking to oneself for motivation, believing in one's abilities to induce command of the game, or visualizing one's movements to optimize flow. And more and more amateurs are indeed resorting to mental gymnastics to help them push their own limits. Of course, the fitness industry is quite happy to jump on this bandwagon. Many dubious figures now bill themselves as "mental coaches" or "motivational trainers," even though neither title is based on any kind of recognized certification or degree.

A qualified mental coach will begin a serious sports psychology workup with a diagnosis of the current situation. On what level is the athlete competing? What are her problems, wishes, goals? Only then can appropriate methods be found to improve concentration, coordination or endurance. Through it all, however, athletes must keep one hard fact in mind: physical fitness and mastery of technique and tactics are the overwhelming determinants of success in any sport. No one has ever won a marathon through mental training alone.

Scientific American Mind,
Volume 16, Number 1, 2005

Extreme Sports, Sensation Seeking and the Brain

"Type T" personalities push themselves
to the brink of death for the neuronal rush or
to relieve the ennui of modern life

GLENN ZORPETTE

Deep underwater off Grand Cayman Island, I hovered over an ethereal, sandy tableau that sloped steeply away into an inky void. I had dipped into the upper edge of a twilight world seen by relatively few scuba divers, where the abundant hard corals of shallower water begin giving way to a sparser assortment in which large soft corals predominate. Off to my left, a big eagle ray flapped slowly and serenely, its white-spotted black body undulating against the dark-blue background of the abyss.

I glanced at my depth gauge, saw that it read 200 feet (61 meters) and grinned. Breathing a mixture of helium, oxygen and nitrogen from two of the four large tanks strapped to my body, I was beyond the depths that could be visited safely with ordinary scuba equipment and techniques. I was oddly, ineffably elated.

Over the previous eight days I had made half a dozen dives to depths between 52 and 58 meters, to satisfy the requirements of two courses in technical diving. During all those dives I breathed ordinary air, and the high nitrogen content sometimes brought on a strange mix of drunkenness tinged with a vague unease, as though different parts of my brain were in a struggle over whether enjoyment or terror should prevail. This nitrogen narcosis was most intense on the deepest dives. As a reward for enduring them, my instructor, Kirk Krack, suggested a final dive with the much less narcotic helium mixture, so that I could experience the joy of being deep underwater with a clear head.

As it happened, the day of the dive was my 37th birthday. But down in that sunken realm, I felt very much like an adolescent boy getting away with something naughty. Looking around, I became an awestruck visitor to a beautiful, forbidden zone, to which only knowledge, experience and technology could grant access. I achieved a kind of focus that only the desire to survive can instill. The cares, petty worries and job stresses of my terrestrial life were, at least for the moment, in a different world.

I'm not alone. Fueled in part by television, a few glossy magazines and some best-selling nonfiction books, extreme sports have managed to seize and hang on to at least a sliver of the popular attention span. The various coteries of practitioners are overwhelmingly male, as is the larger group that follows the exploits of the top stars.

Psychologists view an affinity for extreme sports as a form of sensation seeking, a category whose other entries are mostly disturbing—alcoholism, drug addiction, compulsive gambling, reckless driving, and some kinds of violent criminality and suicide. Indeed, as recently as the 1950s the profession saw sport parachutists, mountain climbers and other adrenaline junkies as indulging self-destructive urges and unconscious death wishes.

Because their passions do not disrupt society, extreme sports enthusiasts have not had nearly the kind of scientific scrutiny that has been focused on other sensation seekers. Nevertheless, in recent years a few psychologists have come up with more sophisticated explanations for the behavior, ones that are now largely free of references to pathology.

Temple University psychologist Frank Farley, for instance, identifies people who crave novelty and thrills as "Type Ts." Farley also labels them as either intellectual (examples include mental iconoclasts such as Albert Einstein and Pablo Picasso) or—in the case of extreme sports devotees—physical. Farley further classifies extreme sports people as "Type T positive physical" to separate them from, say, barroom brawlers, whom he refers to as "Type T negative physical."

Farley and other psychologists have also distinguished a variety of motivations that prompt people to take up this kind of activity. There is the old saw about feeling most alive when closest to death; melodramatic though that may sound, many participants do speak of heightened awareness and stimulation accompanying a dangerous excursion. More generally, most want to know the limits of their mettle and experience deep satisfaction after pushing themselves to a new milestone.

Another factor for some is a feeling of restlessness or even rebellion in the First World societies whose endless suburbs, comfortable routines, ubiquitous television and often oppressive liability laws seem to have created a way of life that is safe but deadening and culturally homogeneous and bland.

A minority of people, mainly otherwise mild-mannered men, appear to pursue extreme sports mainly to impress their friends or co-workers. And a smaller group of "counterphobics" engage in risky pastimes out of an almost obsessive agenda to confront deeply rooted fears. But other than these categories of people, participants report experiences pleasurable enough to compel them to engage in the activity over and over again. This fact suggests an underlying neurochemical basis for the behavior, and indeed neuroscientists have begun identifying one.

Their studies have so far emphasized three neurotransmitters, small molecules that carry signals from cell to cell in the brain. Signaling occurs when a change in electrical potential causes one cell to release a neurotransmitter, which quickly defuses to a receptor on an adjacent cell. The receptor is a protein on the surface of a cell that binds specifically to the neurotransmitter. Each neurotransmitter can combine with different types of receptors, which react characteristically when they bind to the neurotransmitter.

The three neurotransmitters implicated in sensation seeking are dopamine, which is associated with intensely pleasurable feelings; serotonin, linked to many types of extreme behavior; and norepinephrine, a key player in the "fight or flight" response. The levels of all three in the brain are regulated by an enzyme called monoamine oxidase (MAO). Dennis L. Murphy, a neuroscientist at the National Institute of Mental Health, found in 1980 that sensation seekers generally have low levels of MAO. Because MAO helps to break down and inactivate levels of dopamine, serotonin and norepinephrine, low MAO means higher levels of those neurotransmitters. And according to one speculative theory, people with high resting rates of the neurotransmitters need comparatively more stimulation to become aroused.

More recent theories have focused on the levels of the brain's receptors, rather than of the neurotransmitters. According to Kenneth Blum, a psychopharmacologist, the levels of two of the five receptors for dopamine are key "controlling factors" in sensation seeking. He says that people who have smaller numbers of these two receptors, designated D_2 and D_4, must spend more time stimulating the receptors with thrill-released dopamine to get a reasonable ration of excitement in their lives. Serotonin is important, too, he adds, because it stimulates the release of neurotransmitters called endorphins, which inhibit others called GABA, which finally allows the release of more dopamine.

Men are far more likely to have this neural need for excitement; the reason is a result of hundreds of thousands of years of evolution. Some psychologists contend that sensation seekers were crucial to primitive societies, because they could be counted on to reconnoiter areas no one else would visit, taste things that no one else would eat and pursue animals others would just as soon let alone.

Much of the thinking on the psychobiology of extreme sports is speculative, because most studies of the brain chemistry of humans are done indirectly. Moreover, there isn't even much agreement on what constitutes an extreme sport. But a thumbnail review such as the one offered below turns up a few consistencies. One is that most extreme sports evolved from existing pastimes as top practitioners pushed beyond the confines of the sport, oftentimes by borrowing equipment or methods from related disciplines.

These sketches might therefore be seen as snapshots of a work in progress. Its creators may think they are merely satisfying their own urges, but science suggests they are using the expanded technological opportunities of the late 20th century to respond to ancient, evolutionary motives. In time, these people—male and female—may give us more insights into the brain, evolution and why men are the way they are.

Technical Diving

What it is: A form of scuba diving that exploits technologies and techniques from commercial, cave and military diving to permit excursions to depths below 39 meters.

Number of regular U.S. participants: Roughly 10,000.

Specific dangers of the activity: Decompression illness; oxygen toxicity; drowning after becoming lost in an enclosed environment, such as a cave or wreck.

Fatality rate: In 1998, 10 or 11 U.S. divers perished during technical dives, according to Joel Dovenbarger, vice president of medical services for Divers Alert Network in Durham, N.C.

The "Mount Everest" of the activity: The sunken ocean liner *Andrea Doria*, which sits in 73 meters of water off Nantucket Island, Mass. Even veteran divers have been overcome by the combination of strong currents, poor visibility, cold water and the wreck's labyrinthine interior, which presents many opportunities to become disoriented. (In the summer of 1998 three divers died on the wreck.)

Legendary figure, deceased: Sheck Exley, a veteran of 4,000 cave dives, died in 1994 during a 298-meter descent into a vertical cave in east-central Mexico.

Legendary figure, alive: Tom Mount, a cave-diving pioneer and chairman of the International Association of Nitrox and Technical Divers. Mount has logged more than 10,000 dives, including an excursion to 145 meters off Andros Island in the Bahamas.

Free Solo Climbing

What it is: Rock climbing without safety ropes or any other protective hardware.

Number of regular U.S. participants: Fewer than 2,000, estimates Jed Williamson, president of Sterling College and editor of *Accidents in North American Mountaineering*, an annual report published by the American Alpine Club.

Specific dangers of the activity: Falling.

Fatality rate: About one every three or four years, according to Williamson.

The "Mount Everest" of the activity: Yosemite National Park's Half Dome, a 600-meter climb.

Legendary figure, deceased: Dan Osman, who died in 1998 while attempting a roped free fall from Yosemite's Leaning Tower, a 365-meter-high granite wall.

Legendary figure, alive: Peter Croft, whose 450-meter ascent of the Astroman route on Washington Column in Yosemite still has not been repeated.

Extreme Skiing

What it is: A combination of mountaineering and skiing, it involves descents of high, rugged, very steep slopes reachable only by climbing.

Number of regular U.S. participants: 15, according to Dean Cummings, winner of the 1995 World Extreme Skiing Championship. A related activity, free skiing, includes other forms of aggressive skiing and has roughly 5,000 devotees in the U.S., according to Lhotse C. Merriam, vice president of the International Free Skiers Association.

Specific dangers of the activity: Being buried by an avalanche; falling while climbing or skiing.

Fatality rate: Between 1993 and 1997, 25 "backcountry" skiers were killed in the U.S., according to Jim Frankenfield, director of the Cyberspace Snow and Avalanche Center; almost all could probably be considered free skiers.

The "Mount Everest" of the activity: Mount McKinley's Wickersham Wall, with its 4,000-vertical-meter drop and average pitch in excess of 40 degrees.

Legendary figure, deceased: Trevor Petersen, who died in 1996 in an avalanche in Chamonix, France.

Legendary figure, alive: Doug Coombs, winner of the World Extreme Skiing Championship in 1991 and 1993.

BASE Jumping

What it is: Parachuting off tall buildings, bridges, sheer cliffs and the like, often at night. (BASE stands for "buildings, antennas, spans and earth.")

Number of regular U.S. participants: Fewer than 1,000.

Specific dangers of the activity: "Overdelaying" opening of the chute.

Fatality rate: Approximately 45 people have died since 1980, according to Frank Gambalie, an avid jumper.

The "Mount Everest" of the activity: Many newcomers strive to earn their "BASE award" by making at least one jump off an object in each of the four categories.

Legendary figure, deceased: Bob Neely, who died in 1998 jumping off a 381-meter tower in Lee County, Florida.

Legendary figure, alive: Dennis McGlynn, who has made close to 800 jumps, including leaps from cable cars, lighthouses and smokestacks.

Downhill Mountain Biking

What it is: Time-trial race, generally down a ski slope in summer. Average time is about five minutes, during which competitors can hit speeds as high as 105 kilometers per hour (65 miles per hour).

Number of regular U.S. participants: A total of 4,666 people competed in the six national championship races held last year by the National Off-Road Bicycle Association (4,088 of these competitors were men).

Specific dangers of the activity: Losing control of the bike; being thrown from it.

Fatality rate: Fewer than one a year, according to Patrice Quintero, communications director for NORBA.

The "Mount Everest" of the activity: The Kamikaze on Mammoth Mountain in Mammoth Lakes, Calif. ˙

Legendary figure, deceased: Jake Watson, who was thrown from his bike during a practice run near Bakersfield, Calif., on March 12 of this year [1999] and died after hitting a boulder.

Legendary figure, alive: Missy Giove. She was World Cup champion in 1996 and 1997, world champion in 1994 and the top finisher in nine U.S. races. (The premier male rider is John Tomac, who has won more races than any other competitor.)

Scientific American Presents Men: The Scientific Truth, Summer 1999

GEAR AND TECHNIQUE

Going through the Motions

*The field of biomechanics demonstrates
how the scientific study of sport and the training
of athletes are often at odds*

DELIA K. CABE

A pitcher's windup. A gymnast's dismount. A swimmer's glide. Basic principles of physics govern these movements. Biomechanics, the discipline that studies them, tries to reduce the heroic grace and power of the athlete to its most essential constituents. A medal-winning dash to the finish line is not a triumph of the human spirit but a product of mass times acceleration. Biomechanists are the practitioners of the most fundamental science of sport. If only center of gravity, velocity and acceleration could be deduced with sufficient precision, a winning performance might be engineered from first principles. In such a world, the coach would become more cheerleader than trainer.

This vision follows logically from an understanding of the research endeavors of biomechanics. Paradoxically, these premier scientists of sport would be unlikely to articulate such a grand scheme for their doings. Many biomechanical experts, in fact, are having to fight a defensive rearguard action to justify the relevance of their jobs.

In the real world of coaching elite athletes, biomechanists don't get much respect, despite the 35-year history of the field. Trainers do consider biomechanical analyses, often based on digitized videos of an athlete's performance. For instance, a biomechanist might suggest the best position for a volleyball player to place the arms in relation to the shoulders so that the deltoid and pectoral muscles produce the most force. Still, the biomechanists' recommendations are often relatively minor input in an overall coaching strategy.

No Time for Bound Vortices

Why have scientists schooled in the physics and engineering of athletic movement fallen into such disrepute? To begin with, biomechanical experts are lousy communicators, says Benjamin F. Johnson, director of the biomechanics and ergonomics lab at Georgia State University. The significance of their research is hidden under a blanket of scientific jargon. Explanations of the Magnus effect and bound vortices have yet to prove inspirational to either coaches or their charges. To many coaches, biomechanical analysis smacks of academic esoterica—a set of numerical abstractions divorced entirely from the intense psychological focus and drive that distinguish select athletes from mere mortals. "[Scientists] measure only things they can measure, and therefore if they can't measure something, in their minds it doesn't exist," says Richard Quick, head coach of the U.S. women's swim team.

Whether superstitious or simply cautious, athletes and coaches do not want to take a gamble with scientific data that suggest changes to a technique that has produced winners again and again. Like any science, biomechanics continues to evolve, and a recommendation to do one thing one year may be completely reversed a few years hence. Swimming provides an ideal example. Theories about the underlying physics—and consequent suggestions on stroke technique derived from the science—have shifted back and forth in a way that exasperates some coaches.

Throwing Out Newton

Until 1969 scientists thought that the propulsion from a swimmer's arm stroke could be explained by Newton's third law. Pulling the arm through the water with a certain force provoked an opposite force of equal intensity, as per Newton, lending the swimmer the necessary forward propulsion. Extrapolating from theory, coaches at the time told athletes to pull their arm straight back in a stroke they thought would elicit the most oomph—the greatest Newtonian countershove—from the viscous medium they travel through.

What remained perplexing, however, was that underwater video taken of the best swimmers showed that their arms did not pull directly back. Instead they traced a curvilinear path as they moved along the lane. James "Doc" Counsilman, a prominent biomechanist and the Indiana University swim coach of Olympic champion Mark Spitz, was originally one of those who had cited Newton's third law in his seminal 1968 work, *The Science of Swimming*. But after having photographed what appeared to be the circular strokes of competitive swimmers with lights attached to their hands in a darkened pool, Counsilman reevaluated his views. How could the body be propelled forward by a Newtonian counterforce if the hands were swerving all over the place?

In a 1971 paper Counsilman presented a new theory, also borrowed from classical physics, that shocked the swimming community. He suggested that Bernoulli's principle, which produces the lift forces that keep an airplane aloft, played a big role in explaining a swimmer's propulsion along a pool lane. Applied to swimming, it means that water travels faster over the knuckles than the palm and that the difference in pressure between the two sides of the hand generates a propulsive force.

For nearly three decades thereafter, Counsilman's views became the received wisdom, and elite swimming coaches taught their students to slice their hand through the water, emphasizing lateral and vertical motions instead of a straight pull back, all maneuvers designed to enhance lift.

The theory seemed enticing and elegant— except that more and more evidence suggests that it's wrong. Critics have said that the surface area of the hands and feet are neither large enough nor curved enough to produce the necessary lift to move a swimmer through the water. More recently, the case against Bernoulli has grown stronger as scientists have developed precise tools for modeling the physical dynamics of the hand and forearm in water.

The U.S. Olympic Committee has provided the funds for Barry Bixler, an aerospace engineer at Honeywell Engines and Systems in Phoenix, to help resolve some of these questions by deploying the computational fluid dynamic modeling tools that he uses in his day job to simulate the way air races through aircraft engines. Bixler, who works with Scott Riewald of USA Swimming, the sport's national governing body, has used the software to show how water behaves on the forearm and hand. The software, which has often been compared to a wind tunnel in a computer, reveals the velocity at which water flows over the limb, pressure changes in the water and the ways these phenomena affect lift and drag forces.

In Bixler's model, the thin boundary layer of water flowing over the surface of a hand and forearm pulled away before it could pass completely around the limb. The computational simulation indicates that the Bernoulli effect does not explain how a swimmer does laps, because the Swiss physicist's mathematics assumed that lift forces would not be produced if air, water or any fluid in the boundary layer separated from the surface of the body around which it flowed.

Astonishingly, these findings take biomechanists back to the original 1960s thesis of Counsilman and others. The hand behaves like Newton's paddle, not Bernoulli's airplane wing. When it puts pressure against water's resistive medium, the hand provokes a counterforce that accounts for the propulsion. Many of those who train swimmers poolside from day to day have witnessed this debate with a growing sense of bafflement. "This has upset some coaches who took a long time accepting the lift theory of propulsion [based on the Bernoulli effect] and who now feel the rug has been pulled out from under them," says Ernest W. Maglischo, a biomechanist and former swimming coach at Arizona State University.

The case is not closed. Some lift still seems to be involved in propulsion. Moreover, Counsilman's original inductive insight, which prompted the shift from Newton to Bernoulli, holds: good swimmers do not stroke straight back but in a somewhat circular pattern, perhaps because they can achieve a longer pull and thus a greater stroke length.

The change in explanation does, however, raise questions about the teaching conventions of the past few decades. Once Counsilman conceived of a swimmer's hand and forearm as a kind of lift-driven wing, instructors taught students to emphasize slice-like strokes that may have led to performance inefficiencies. Maglischo writes in a new version of a swimming textbook he authored that the Bernoulli diversion has caused stroke mechanics to seem "far more complex than they really are. And as a result, techniques for teaching competitive swimming strokes have been needlessly complicated." For his part, Bixler says that if further research confirms these initial findings, a less pronounced sideways motion during the stroke might be ideal. As a good scientist, though, Bixler begs to dither: "Borrowing from a well-known TV show," he says, "that might not be my final answer."

And that may also be just the point. Bixler's research demonstrates how difficult it is for biomechanics to get any hard answers that spring from a foundation of real science. For instance, it takes enormous resources to simulate the complexities of the swimmer's interaction with the water. The computational fluid dynamics analysis provides the most accurate information to date on the dynamics of swimming. But the simulations necessary for precisely modeling the set of variables in Bixler's analysis took six months to run.

One area of athletics in which biomechanics has gained some grudging acceptance is in the design of equipment and sports garb. Although it is a sport relatively free of technological encumbrances, swimming has spawned a recent controversy, not over the effectiveness of teaching a particular technique but over the possibility that a new type of swimsuit is perhaps too good at improving performance. Both Speedo and Adidas have introduced full-body swimsuits made from more advanced materials than the ones with shorter legs and arms worn in the Atlanta Olympics. No one objected back then because they did not perceive the more circumscribed suits as a radical change. The full-length version was harder to ignore and coincided with a spate of record breaking.

Sharkskin Suits

The weave of nylon, Lycra and polyester in the Speedo suit's fabric forms fine ridges that imitate a shark's skin. The manufacturer claims that the suit, which

Keeping Abreast of New Technology

Research by biomechanists and materials scientists at Australia's University of Wollongong may presage the advent of a lingerie department at your local computer store. The researchers have concocted an intelligent sports bra that should make participating in athletics more comfortable for women. A computer microchip will control polymer sensors woven into the Smart Bra, directing the fabric to tighten or relax in response to breast movement. Kelly-Ann Bowles, a doctoral student in biomechanics at the university, is conducting trials to measure breast motion, strap and cup strain, and breast pain across different sizes. "What we need to find is a maximum level of breast motion acceptable and then calculate the strain associated with that," Bowles says.

Bowles and her co-workers, Julie Steele, head of the Biomechanics Research Laboratory, and Gordon Wallace, director of the Intelligent Polymer Research Institute, are hoping that a brainy bra will encourage more women to compete in sports—and prevent the injuries, such as broken clavicles, that are associated with large breasts. Bras as they are designed now, Bowles says, also put pressure on women's shoulders, leading to troughlike strap marks and, possibly, pinched nerves that can affect sensation in their pinkies. The researchers' investigations have just begun, as have their discussions with the Australian bra company Berlei. If the Smart Bra does come to market, which Bowles hopes will happen in the next two years, "software support" will take on a whole new meaning.

—Naomi Lubick

costs between $100 and $300, reduces drag and enhances performance by 3 percent. The operative word is "enhance," and therein lies the controversy. FINA, swimming's international governing body, has approved the high-tech suit for competition. But others, including USA Swimming's national team director, Dennis Pursley, say that it violates FINA guidelines, which preclude any accoutrements that give a competitor an advantage. The Australian Olympic Committee asked the Court of Arbitration for Sport in Switzerland to determine whether the suit breaks the rules, and the court ruled in FINA's favor. Some swimmers think the suit provides an unfair advantage, although other observers say that the suit does nothing more than provide a psychological edge by boosting a swimmer's confidence.

In some athletes' eyes the disservice has to do less with performance enhancement and more with supply. Last spring, Swimming Canada and USA Swimming barred the suits at their Olympic swimming trials because of limited availability. Speedo has announced that it will provide the suit to all swimmers regardless of sponsorship in the Sydney Games, just days after Olympic gold medalist Kieren Perkins of Australia expressed dissatisfaction because the suits were not easy to get. Acceptance of the full-body suits demonstrates that when biomechanists really do make a good case, the kind of academic debates that pit Newton against Bernoulli fade as quickly as the turbulent vortices in a swimmer's wake.

Scientific American Presents: Building the Elite Athlete, Fall 2000

Asphalt Acrobats

To pull off spectacular tricks, crafty skateboarders
bend the laws of physics

PEARL TESLER

In June 1999 professional skateboarder Tony Hawk made history by performing the impossible. Egged on by a wildly enthusiastic crowd at San Francisco's X Games, he nailed the first recorded "900"—a horizontal midair twist of two and a half revolutions (900 degrees)—high above the huge U-shaped "half-pipe" that launched him toward the California sky.

Starting at the right-hand top of the U, Hawk plunged down inside the half-pipe to gain speed, then vaulted up and out of the opposite wall. Airborne and parallel to the ground, he immediately tucked his body, clutched the skateboard and spun two and a half rotations—finishing quickly enough that he could again extend his legs and push the board back against the left wall of the U before crashing down into the cement pipe's trough. To skateboard fanatics, the 900 was so difficult a maneuver that it seemed to be beyond an invisible barrier. It had eluded Hawk's efforts for 10 long years.

What made the 900 possible? Watching skaters like Hawk soar, twirl and swoop in a sophisticated blur of limbs, the real question seems to be: What makes any of it possible? Executed at top speeds, skateboard tricks can be difficult to follow, let alone understand.

It seems that skaters are defying the laws of physics. But the fact is, they're just cleverly exploiting the forces of nature. Every maneuver a skateboarder makes takes advantage of the fundamental physical principles that govern motion in virtually every sport: speed, momentum, rotation, gravity and good old muscle power. Analyzing skaters' brazen acrobatics unveils the scientific mysteries that allow an ice skater to spin, a diver to twist, a gymnast to tumble and a freestyle skier to catch "big air."

The Ollie

Before the 900 was even a glimmer in Tony Hawk's eye, there was the ollie. Invented in the late 1970s by Florida skater Alan "Ollie" Gelfand, the ollie is skateboarding's primordial trick, the foundation on which most other tricks are based. In its simplest form, the ollie is a jump that allows street skaters to skip up onto sidewalks, hop over obstacles and leap across urban chasms.

What amazes onlookers is that the board seems to lift magically with the skater's rising feet throughout the jump. Many people assume that the skateboard is somehow attached to the skater's shoes. It's not. Equally perplexing is that to make the skateboard soar up, a skater first stomps *down* on it. A step-by-step look at this paradoxical trick reveals the secret: skillfully controlled rotation of the skateboard.

The ollie begins explosively. A skater rolling along on flat ground places his front foot in the middle of the board and his rear foot on the tail. He drops into a crouch, which lowers his center of mass (the point where his weight is most concentrated). As the skater approaches the obstacle to be jumped, he throws up his arms and torso, accelerating his body upward before his feet begin to rise. (Starting with a lower center of mass gives the body more distance over which to accelerate before the skater's feet leave the ground. The height of any skateboard jump comes from this upward acceleration; the greater the acceleration, the higher the jump.)

As the skater's body streaks upward in launch, he stomps down hard on the skateboard's tail with his rear foot. The great force on the tail causes the front of the board to rear up. The board rotates backward around the rear wheel, nose lifting up into the air like a rising jet plane.

The downward stomp on the tail, however, causes it to strike the ground—hard—a fraction of a second later. The tail then bounces back up. Now the skateboard is fully in the air, rotating forward again; the front tip begins to come down while the back tip moves up. If left to its own devices, the skateboard would eventually flip tail over nose. But the airborne skater uses his feet to control the rotation, sliding his front foot forward to drag the nose of the board upward with his rising leap. Aided by the extra friction of sandpaperlike grip tape on the skateboard's top surface, this dragging motion keeps the skater's front foot in constant contact with the skateboard. Meanwhile the skater lifts his rear foot to get it out of the way of the rising tail. If he times these motions just right, his feet and the board will rise in perfect unison, seemingly stuck together.

At the top of the jump, the skater levels the board with his feet to stop its rotation. Now at their maximum height, skater and skateboard begin to fall together under the influence of gravity. To cushion the impact of landing, the skater drops his arms and bends his knees. In under a second, the ollie is over.

Frontside 180

After skaters master the ollie, they begin to add aerial maneuvers. One favorite is begun by speeding forward off a curb, or off the top of a short flight of stairs, and launching straight out into the air. Once in midflight, the skater rotates the board and his legs a full 180 degrees before touching down on the ground.

Skaters call this a frontside 180; a physics student might call it impossible.

At first glance, the aerial turn seems to violate a basic law of physics, the conservation of angular momentum, which states that if you aren't rotating, the only way to start is with the help of a twisting force—a torque. But a skater already in the air has nothing to push against to create the needed torque. The only force that acts on someone in flight is gravity, and gravity can only make a person fall. It can't make you spin. So how does a skater create rotation out of thin air?

To generate the torque he needs, the skater borrows a trick from the amazing housecat. The lore that cats always land on their feet may not be strictly true, but it's also more than just talk. To right themselves while falling, cats do exactly what the stair-jumping skater must do: rotate while keeping their angular momentum constant at zero. Here's how it works: A cat falling with its back to the ground thrusts its back legs straight out behind its body. It simultaneously tucks its front legs. Extending the rear legs increases their rotational inertia—their tendency to stay straight and resist spinning. This shift of the hind legs creates a small torque that is transmitted through the cat's body. Because the front legs are tucked, their rotational inertia is relatively small; it takes only a small torque to rotate them. The result, very useful for the cat, is that the torque traveling through the cat's torso twists its front legs down toward the ground.

Using its muscles to stop the front legs' rotation when pointing closer toward the ground, the cat generates torque that can travel back through its body and help bring the hind legs around, too. With enough falling time, a cat can ratchet itself around by repeating these opposing twist motions, until both sets of feet are pointed down for the landing.

The torque needed for the frontside 180 is created in much the same way.

Once airborne, the skater thrusts his arms out wide. This increases his upper body's rotational inertia, making it harder to turn. He then throws his outspread arms in one direction, creating torque through the body that twists his legs (and skateboard) in the opposite direction. A nice sweep of the arms can cause a full 180-degree twist of the feet. Because the two rotations cancel each other out, the skater's total angular momentum stays the same—zero—and the law of conservation of momentum remains unbroken.

Big Air

Never is a skater's instinctive mastery of physics more apparent, or more necessary, than when she is skating in a big, foreboding half-pipe, a structure sometimes called a vert ramp. Lay a sheet of paper on the table, curl the edges so they point straight up, and you have a rough model of a vert ramp, so called because the topmost sections are perfectly vertical. Actual vert ramps are usually about 12 feet tall.

Once skaters learn how to dive and climb, traversing the trough of the ramp on each pass, they begin to contemplate an alluring daredevil move: getting enough momentum in the downswing to vault them up past the top of the far wall. Once in the air, they rotate a half-turn and skate back down the wall. Good skaters can roll down one side and up the other, return, and then do it again and again, while getting a little air at the top of each ascent.

It may seem that skaters in vert ramps are simply riding back and forth. But—although their parents may disagree—they're really working. Physics holds that when you're at a certain height above the ground—say, atop a vert ramp—you have a store of potential energy proportional to this height. You can convert this energy into kinetic energy, or motion, by rolling down the ramp and collect it back as potential energy when you roll back up the far side. But to make it back up to the top, a skater has to compensate for the energy lost to air resistance and the friction of the wheels on the cement half-pipe by adding energy. And if she wants to rise above the ramp—necessary for an airborne turn—she has to add even more energy. This means work.

On flat ground, the conventional skating method for adding energy is to push off the ground with one foot. But in vert ramps, skaters use a more elegant method called pumping. To pump, a skater crouches down while traversing the flat bottom of the ramp. Then, as she enters the upward curve, called the transition, she straightens her legs and rises. By repeating this motion each time she passes through the transition, a skater gives herself incremental boosts of speed that allow her to rise above the ramp wall.

Paul Doherty, a physicist at the Exploratorium museum in San Francisco, explains that this kind of pumping is identical to the pumping you do to go higher on a playground swing, in which you lift your ankles and feet up and forward as they pass through the bottom of the arc, then drop them at the top of the arc. "When you lift your legs at the bottom, your muscles have to work extra hard against the gravity force and the centrifugal force," Doherty says. "The energy you exert by lifting your legs against these forces makes you go higher and faster." The same principle, of course, applies to skaters in vert ramps, but instead of lifting their legs, they lift their whole bodies. So, if pumping makes skaters go higher, the next natural question is, Just how high can they go?

Skaters know that big air—rising high above the top edge of the ramp—is partly a function of ramp size. The current record holder, Danny Way, rose 16.5 feet out of an exceptionally tall, 18-foot ramp assembled by the DC Shoe Company at an airstrip near the California-Mexico border. Large ramps are more forgiving of the high-flying skater, because their larger transitions ease the shift from vertical to horizontal motion. And because the greater speeds they create mean greater centrifugal force to push against, the large ramps also make pumping even more fruitful. But at some point, the energy added with each pump can't compensate for the energy lost to wind resistance. The upshot? Height records will continue to climb, but each successive inch will come at a steeper price.

900 Degrees . . . and Beyond?

By now it might be clear how legendary Tony Hawk manages to do the 900—and how stunning the maneuver is. Hawk must create a strong enough pump to launch himself sufficiently high above the vert ramp to have time to spin 900 degrees. And he must find a way to create the necessary catlike torque to twist his body two and a half times.

The truth is that to pull off a megatrick like the 900, Hawk also has to use a bit of catlike sneakiness. The two seconds he is airborne isn't quite enough time to fabricate the required rotation for 900 degrees of spin. Hawk has to leave the ramp already spinning. Then he must parlay this rotational energy into an even faster spin with a technique common to another form of skating—ice skating.

To accomplish their triple lutzes, ice skaters start with a wide sweeping spin, arms and legs extended. In the air, they pull their limbs in. This decreases rotational inertia, causing them to spin faster automatically.

Likewise, before he launches from the top of the ramp, Hawk gives himself a sizable amount of angular momentum. He approaches the top of the ramp with outstretched arms. As he nears the top, he tucks and begins to spin his body, pushing hard on the board to create an angular force. The angular momentum gained in this moment is all he'll have throughout the trick. After he leaves the ramp, he can't get any more.

The moment he is airborne, he speeds up the spin by jutting one outstretched arm high over his head, adding rotational torque. He drops the other arm to hold the skateboard (there's not enough friction between his feet and the board to drag it along during this superfast spin). Placing his arms in line with his body—his axis of rotation—speeds his spin, allowing him to squeeze in two and a half rotations in two seconds. These rotations are an act of faith. Hawk is no longer in control; at best, his control is limited. Turning quickly, body almost parallel to the ground, he twice completely loses sight of the ramp from which he has launched and onto which he must land. Only by throwing his arms wide after the second full spin can he slow his rotation enough to "spot" his landing. As the skateboard touches down, he absorbs his momentum by collapsing into a deep crouch, readying himself for a controlled yet jubilant landing at the bottom.

Hawk had hardly rolled to a stop after performing his miracle 900 when the buzz began: Could he do three full spins, a 1080? In an on-line chat room interview, Hawk unambiguously put the speculation to rest: "I don't have any desire to spin any further." Hawk describes each punishing attempt at the 900 as a potential trip to the hospital. Now 32 years old, he seems happy to leave the 1080 to younger, sprier disciples.

If you ask Jake Phelps, editor of *Thrasher* magazine, the skateboarder's bible, a 1080 is a definite, if delayed, possibility. "Someone may do it," he comments, "but not for a long time." Skateboarding, Phelps continues, is in a state of perpetual evolution, constantly consuming and reinventing itself as new tricks become old hat: "The greatest thing about skating is it changes every day. The first time I saw somebody ollie on the street I was like, 'No way!' But now every kid can get on a board and make an ollie. Today's impossible trick is just cannon fodder for the future."

Scientific American Presents: Building the Elite Athlete, Fall 2000 Further Information: News and trick tips can be found on the Web at www.skate boarding.com and in Thrasher *magazine.*

Electronic Skis

MARK FISCHETTI

For decades, skiers slid down snow-covered hills on long rectangular planks. But in the mid-1990s companies began offering skis with an hourglass shape. They turned more easily because they concentrated the skier's weight at the middle of the ski's inside blade edge. The focus makes the ski less likely to slip out of the track that the blade carves as it traverses the inevitable microbumps of snow on any slope. Today "shaped" or "carving" skis dominate the market.

There's a subtle catch, however. The concentrated forces create a strong angular moment within the ski. To maintain structural integrity, the ski must be built with more rigidity. But that means the ski is apt to vibrate, which is annoying and can even lift it off the snow, causing a skier to wipe out.

In the past six years, manufacturers have laid various synthetics in the ski to dampen vibrations. But the most effective option may be piezoelectric fibers, already employed in tennis rackets, which convert vibration, compression or bending energy into electric current. A chip embedded in the ski accumulates, reverses and returns the current, making the fibers expand and contract, countering the angular momentum and creating a smooth, easy turn. A growing number of pro skiers are using piezo designs. "It's a quieter ride," says Joe Cutts, equipment editor for *Ski* magazine. The skis are also "more versatile" in various snow conditions, says Peter Keelty, co-founder of RealSkiers.com.

Unfortunately, chip-controlled, or "active," piezo skis cost about 50 percent more. And some reviewers think the benefits may be lost on recreational skiers, making a noticeable difference only at higher speeds on icy snow. K2, a large ski maker, has dropped its piezo models, which used piezo patches that passively absorbed vibrations rather than a chip for active feedback. Other designers maintain that a smartly devised layer of rubber can provide almost the same benefits at a fraction of the cost.

But Herfried Lammer, senior design engineer at Head Sport AG in Kennelbach, Austria, the piezo leader, says that skiers prefer the electronic glide. "At the end of the day, skiers must like what they feel on the slopes. And they do."

Did You Know

Hot Shoes: Advanced Cerametrics in Lambertville, N.J., is developing self-heated hiking and ski boots powered by piezomaterials in the heel, plus military boots that recharge batteries. It is also devising self-powered fishing lures that emit the sounds of a fish's prey.

Evangelist on Skis: For years, John Howe was director of product development for Head Ski in Baltimore and later consulted for other ski equipment giants. But today the mechanical engineer works from his Waterford, Me., home, annually handcrafting 50 to 100 pairs of a radical product he calls the Claw. It has a rubber layer that he claims dampens vibrations more than any other design. Reviewers say it is superb on icy New England slopes but can be tough sledding in soft snow. Howe sees many commercial innovations as hype. He also sells a book, *The New Skiing Mechanics,* which extensively describes the forces encountered during skiing as it evangelizes the Claw.

Tennis Elbow?: Head Sport first deployed piezomaterials in tennis rackets, to reduce vibrations in the handle after hitting a ball. In July 2002 Werner Zirngibl of the Institute of Orthopedics and Sports Medicine in Munich gave piezo rackets to 55 recreational players who were being treated for either temporary or chronic tennis elbow. After six weeks of regular play, enthusiasts with a chronic condition found little or no relief, but those who had transient pain reported significant improvement.

DURING A TURN, a skier's weight presses down near the ski's center while the snow's reactive force pushes up along the ski's inside edge. The offset creates an angular moment in the ski's top layer that tends to lift the edge from the snow [single ski, left], which the skier must resist to prevent a skid. The moment changes throughout the turn, setting up vibrations that the skier feels as "chatter"—bumping and downslope slippage.

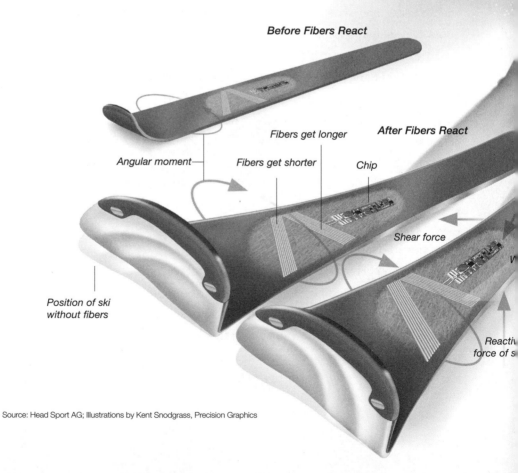

Before Fibers React

Fibers get longer

After Fibers React

Angular moment

Fibers get shorter

Chip

Shear force

Position of ski
without fibers

Reactiv
force of s

Source: Head Sport AG; Illustrations by Kent Snodgrass, Precision Graphics

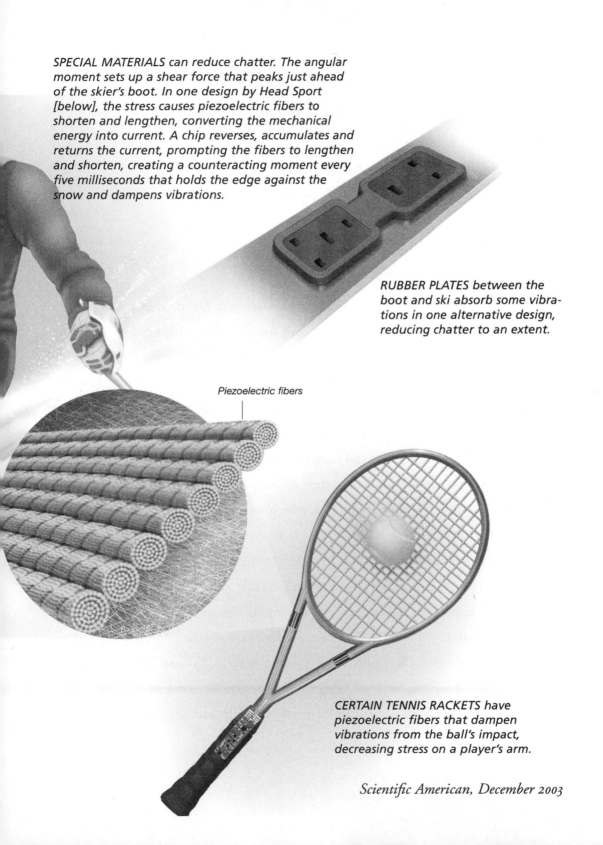

SPECIAL MATERIALS can reduce chatter. The angular moment sets up a shear force that peaks just ahead of the skier's boot. In one design by Head Sport [below], the stress causes piezoelectric fibers to shorten and lengthen, converting the mechanical energy into current. A chip reverses, accumulates and returns the current, prompting the fibers to lengthen and shorten, creating a counteracting moment every five milliseconds that holds the edge against the snow and dampens vibrations.

RUBBER PLATES between the boot and ski absorb some vibrations in one alternative design, reducing chatter to an extent.

Piezoelectric fibers

CERTAIN TENNIS RACKETS have piezoelectric fibers that dampen vibrations from the ball's impact, decreasing stress on a player's arm.

Scientific American, December 2003

The Olympian's New Clothes

*High-tech apparel may determine
who takes home the gold*

FRANK VIZARD

Drug use may be the most prominent controversy surrounding this summer's [2004] Olympic Games in Athens. But the second burning question concerns an entirely legal approach to getting the winning edge: namely, whether or not form-fitting fast-suits made from high-tech fabrics will decide which athletes bring home a medal. These new garments will be most visible in high profile events such as swimming, but rowers and cyclists are sporting them as well. Although to the casual observer the suits might bring to mind costumes for the next *Spiderman* movie, they are less about good looks and more about their ability to reduce drag and thereby increase speed. In events in which the difference between gold and bronze is measured in tenths of a second, the fast suit an athlete wears may be the difference between winning a medal or not.

Manufacturers have devoted considerable energy to developing various approaches to reducing drag. Nowhere is this competition more intense than in swimming. These days, anyone who shows up at the pool in a pair of tiny trunks is a loser. Fast suits are de rigueur. Speedo, Tyr and Nike all produce them but the big battle will be between the two market leaders, Speedo and Tyr, because both companies have adopted different approaches to moving through water quickly.

In the showdown of the suits, bettors might put their money on Speedo because it has the most experience in producing fast suits and because U.S. swimmer Michael Phelps, heavily favored to bring home a sack of medals, will be wearing one. The Speedo Fastskin FSII suit Phelps is using in Athens is a substantial improvement over Speedo's first-generation suit used at the Games in Sydney, Australia, four years ago. "The original Fastskin was too restrictive," says Lenny Krayzelburg, another U.S. swimmer who will be sporting the upgraded Speedo suit. "I can tell the difference," Phelps agrees.

The Fastskin FSII draws on sharks for inspiration and computers for execution. Suit developers noted that although the shark is very streamlined, the shape and texture of its skin varies over its body, corresponding to varying flow conditions. Rough dermal denticles, for example, are found at the nose of a shark while smoother ones are located farther back, reflecting differences in flow at different points on the body.

To study how flow characteristics change as human swimmers move through water, Speedo adapted computational fluid dynamics (CFD) software developed for Formula One race cars. The CFD software was used to create a virtual flume. Next, virtual swimmers were added using CyberFX virtual mannequins—software also used in the making of movies such as *Spiderman* and *The Matrix*. The researchers also conducted tests using real mannequins and athletes in a real flume.

The computer modeling showed that friction drag constitutes up to 29 percent of a swimmer's total drag when underwater—much more than the 10 percent previously thought. To combat friction drag, Speedo used different fabrics arranged to mimic shark skin, altering the pattern according to the stroke used. The company also developed different suits for men and women. One fabric, the Fastskin, works like spandex to compress the body and limit muscle oscillation. Fastskin is designed to reduce friction drag by creating ridges and valleys similar to those on a shark's skin—the water skims over the ridges and skips the drag-inducing valleys in between them. At points where bodies curve, another spandexlike material called Flexskin—joined to the other fabric by low-profile seams—enables greater mobility. Speedo suits also feature titanium-silicon scales on the inner forearm that grip the water better on down strokes. Lastly, rubber bumps across the chest help reduce another type of resistance called pressure drag. The overall effect, Speedo asserts, is a 4 percent reduction in passive drag for men and a 3 percent reduction for women.

But Speedo has it all wrong, according to swimsuit maker Tyr. To go faster in water, you need to increase friction drag, not reduce it, argues David Pendergast, one of the inventors of Tyr's Aqua Shift suit and a professor at the University of Buffalo's Center for Research and Education in Special Environments (CRESE), an institution that counts the U.S. Navy SEALS and NASA among its clients. After studying swimmers in a special donut-shaped pool—a lane-wide loop that enabled continuous swimming—Pendergast found that boosting friction drag lessens two more detrimental types of drag: pressure drag, caused by the shape of the body, and wave drag, the wake created by the swimmer. Friction drag generally occurs at slower speeds, whereas pressure drag and wave drag are encountered as the swimmer moves faster.

To increase the amount of friction drag, the Aqua Shift suit uses three raised rings of equal height, called trip wires, placed where the circumference of the body is greatest—one around the calves, another around the buttocks, and the third around the chest. The overall effect is to keep water closer to the body, thereby minimizing water resistance. The idea isn't new. Prior to the 1994 Winter Olympics, downhill-ski suit maker Spyder developed a suit with raised piping that increased friction drag. The Spyder suit was banned from that Olympics because it was said to offer its wearer an unfair advantage, and the suit was available only to U.S. skiers. The new fast suits, however, are available to all swimmers. Tyr claims its Aqua Shift suit will reduce drag by 10 percent, an achievement that would blow Speedo out of the water. If Michael Phelps' multiple medal hunt is frustrated, it could be by a swimmer wearing a Tyr Aqua Shift suit. On the other hand, if all three spots on the winners' stand go to Speedo wearers, then the donut-shaped pool where Tyr's Aqua Shift suit was born will become symbolic of its failed effort.

Meanwhile, Nike was still working on its Swift Suit design in late July, but it, too, is concentrating on reducing friction drag. Nike may feel more comfortable out of the water though, if only because of its history with a basketball star named Michael and sneakers called Air Jordans. Nike's Swift Suit is an extension of the skintight track and field suit that debuted at the Sydney Olympics. Variations have been developed for speed skating and cycling. Lance Armstrong, the king of the Tour de France cycling race, wears a Nike-made four-ounce jersey that features a lightweight mesh on the back and dimpled material on the shoulders to cut down on drag.

Canada's rowing team will make the most novel use of fast suits at this Olympics. The athletes will wear red and white hooded, sleeveless unisuits, in which all of the seams have been pushed to the front and the fabric itself draws sweat away from the skin so it can quickly evaporate. Nike says the hood alone will reduce drag by 3 percent, which translates to roughly eight feet in a 2,000-meter race. The Canadians will be the only rowers in the Olympics wearing hooded fast suits. (Nike generally prefers sleeveless suits because it believes they offer more freedom for arm movement.)

In the end, fast suits might very well turn their wearers into superheroes of sorts. By the way, if you aspire to Olympic swimmer chic, expect to pay about $400 for the garb. Of course, you can still just shave your body hair like they did in the old days. You just won't look as cool.

scientificamerican.com, August 9, 2004

The Athletic Arms Race

*Does better equipment heighten competition
or ruin the game?*

MIKE MAY

For decades, world records in speed skating were broken by tiny increments, sometimes only one or two hundredths of a second. Suddenly, in 1997, records plummeted by full tenths of a second at a time. Even more startling, virtually unknown skaters were crushing the favorites. The reason: the clap skate. This new piece of equipment carved time off every lap. The skate caused an avalanche of tumbling records at the 1998 Winter Olympics in Nagano, Japan. In the first round of the men's 500 meters, Italian Ermanno Ioriatti set an Olympic record. A few minutes later American Casey FitzRandolph broke Ioriatti's record. Next, Canadian Kevin Overland surpassed FitzRandolph. Finally, Japan's Hiroyasu Shimizu beat Overland. In the men's 5,000 meters, the world record fell three times in less than half an hour.

Spectators could actually hear speed skating change. A traditional skate—a steel blade attached rigidly to a boot's toe and heel—makes a swooshing sound with each stride across the ice. But a passing clap skate creates a rhythmic clatter. The key change is a springloaded hinge that connects the blade to the boot's toe. Beneath the heel, the blade is free to swing away from the boot. When a skater's heel begins to lift up at the end of a stroke, the hinge lets the back of the blade stay on the ice until the foot is raised high. The clap sound comes at the very end of the stroke, when the rear part of the blade snaps back into place. By keeping the blade on the ice longer, a skater gets more push for each stroke, propelling him or her faster. The concept of clap skates had been around for nearly a century, but it made its debut among top skaters at Nagano, spurred on by a host of athletes and scientists from the Faculty of Human Movement Sciences at Free University Amsterdam.

Despite the blazing times, the new skates did not suit everyone. Some skaters took to them fairly easily; others felt like babies learning to walk. "The first time you step onto the ice, you almost fall over," FitzRandolph says. Competitors can't simply strap on the new skates and tear through records. In a few cases, lesser skaters who had quietly trained with the new technology before the Nagano Games had an edge over faster rivals who hadn't gotten used to the equipment soon enough to use it during competition. The skate requires a different stroke, one that pushes more forward and from the toe rather than to the side and from the heel. Although FitzRandolph is comfortable in clap skates now, he admits, "I really like the old skates." But no one dreaming of gold can go back to the previous technology.

The clap skate illustrates a fundamental tension between innovation and sport. Competitors continually look for a technological edge, from faster skates to harder-hitting baseball bats. Likewise, manufacturers persistently enhance equipment in a scramble to win more market share. Governing bodies are thrust into the role of negotiators, hoping to preserve a sport's intended challenges in the face of an athletic arms race.

At first glance, technological advancements seem beneficial, because in most sports incremental improvements can distinguish winners from losers. But taken to the limit, better equipment can reduce or even eliminate the role of athletes' abilities, conditioning and cunning. As Nadine Gelberg, who specializes in sports at Harris Interactive, a market research firm, explains, "Sports are essentially about a challenge, and there's a particular set of skills necessary to meet that challenge. The question is: When does innovation usurp the skills necessary for the challenge?" Tennis could devolve into a serving contest if advanced rackets propelled balls at such blinding speeds that no one could return them. A golf ball designed to self-correct its flight down the fairway would no longer test a golfer's accuracy.

On the other hand, Gelberg points out, technological improvements can widen the participation of youth and women in some sports. And certain advances, such as better running shoes, do indeed simply improve the fair contest between athletes. In essence, sporting equipment should be good but not too good. Technology should not change the basic nature of a game. The real disagreement is over where to draw the line.

Overguarding the Goal

The National Hockey League had to draw a few lines recently after controversy over goalie equipment. The NHL hired Dave Dryden, a star goalie from the 1970s, to help. "Over the years," Dryden says, "the focus of goaltenders had changed from wearing equipment to protect themselves to wearing equipment that fills up the net." Some goalies were wearing jerseys so oversized they looked like capes. Did this make it harder for opposing players to score? "Yes, absolutely," Dryden says. "For the player coming in at the goal and trying to find a spot to shoot the puck, there really weren't a lot of spots left."

In 1998 the NHL ruled that a goalie's equipment could protect only the goalie, not the goal. The rules laid down specific limits for a jersey. It can't be wider than nine inches at the wrist, 29 inches at the chest and 30 inches at the hips. From front to back, it must be no more than 14 inches, and length is limited to a maximum of 32 inches. The changes also limit goalie pant legs to a width of 11 inches at the thigh. As for padding, the rules say only that it must be form-fitting; no bumps or ridges can be added to increase size.

Although NHL officials meant to even out the challenge between scoring and defending, the balance might be swinging to the scorers. "The goalies are saying to me, 'Jeez, Dave, the pucks are coming a lot harder now than they used to,'" Dryden relates. The fastest shots now surpass 100 miles per hour. Dryden expects the league to look soon at the construction of hockey sticks to determine whether they launch the puck too hard. Another technology battle might lie just ahead.

The Happy Nonhooker

Technology really appeared to overshadow an athlete's skill in 1974, when Fred Holmstrom and Daniel Nepela patented a new golf ball. They made the dimples on the poles of the ball shallow, leaving a deeper band of dimples around the equator. If the ball was teed up with the ring of dimples in the vertical plane and then hit, it experienced reduced aerodynamic forces along the undimpled sides, which made it less likely to hook (veer left, for a right-handed golfer) or slice (veer right). The manufacturer, PGA Victor, called the ball the Polara, but the press dubbed it the "happy nonhooker." To be approved for competitive use, golf balls must face Frank Thomas, who runs the U.S. Golf Association's testing facility. Automated driving machines and accomplished golfers hit the Polara and a host of other balls. "The Polara corrected itself in flight," Thomas says. Consequently, the USGA banned it and developed a symmetry standard: a ball must not be made or intentionally modified to have flight properties that differ from those of a spherically symmetrical ball. The ban triggered a series of court battles in which PGA Victor claimed that the

USGA and the Golf Ball Manufacturers Association teamed up to inhibit sales of the new ball. In an out-of-court settlement, the USGA paid the manufacturer $1.4 million, but the ball remained banned.

Thomas explains the need for USGA rules: "If you know exactly where the ball is going to go, instead of going to the next tee you might as well go ahead 250 yards to the middle of the fairway, and start from there." Still, he adds, "we don't want to stifle innovation, because if we specified exactly what every piece of equipment had to look like, golf would be boring as all get-out. So we allow people to innovate, but not to the detriment of the challenge that makes golf so attractive."

Today the USGA tests golf balls indoors on a 70-foot range. An automated system tracks a ball's movement once it is struck, which reveals its initial velocity. A computer simulation then determines the ball's lift and drag properties and calculates how the ball would fly. In a recent batch of tests, the USGA banned a dozen balls out of 1,800 because they would go too far.

To develop long-flight balls, manufacturers examine both design and materials. For example, they can alter the shape and size of a ball's dimples, which can reduce the aerodynamic drag on the ball, making it go farther. Some experiments suggest that hexagon-shaped dimples produce less drag than round ones do. Moreover, materials used in golf balls have changed dramatically, from the boxwood used before the 14th century to today's synthetic core and cover. Manufacturers experiment with many materials in search of ones that are bouncy enough to make a ball travel far but also durable enough for the rigors of the game. Yet they know that their balls must pass Thomas's test, so balls cannot always exploit every technological advantage.

Soaring Spears

Aerodynamic improvements also altered an ancient event, the javelin throw. The wooden rod hadn't changed much until the early 1950s, when American Dick Held made metal javelins. East German Uwe Hohn was the first to break the 100-meter barrier with Held's creation, throwing 104.8 meters. Held's javelins had greater surface area, and the center of gravity was moved back toward the thrower, which created considerable lift. But the spears tended to descend nose-up, often skidding on landing, making it virtually impossible for officials to determine precisely where they hit. Consequently, the International Amateur Athletic Federation instituted a new rule: to be counted, a thrown javelin had to land point-down.

Further complications arose once throwers changed their style. U.S. Olympian Tom Petranoff says, "Everybody thought that throwing a javelin at 30 to 32 degrees was optimum, but when we started throwing them at 25 or 24 degrees, these things went screaming out. I threw a javelin 110 yards. It still blows me away."

Officials decided the new javelins were flying dangerously far. At a Grand Prix final in Rome in 1985, Petranoff threw a javelin that soared to the right and touched down at a winning 92 meters but then bounced and took off again. The projectile shot across the track and speared a board right below the IAAF officials. The next year, the IAAF pushed the allowable center of gravity in a javelin four centimeters forward. Petranoff's throws dropped by 40 feet. The modifications also essentially forced throwers to return to old techniques, in which finesse means less and brute strength means more. Now, Petranoff says, "people with power can get away with murder."

Spaghetti, Anyone?

Technology has also altered the balance of finesse and power in tennis. Anyone who once played the game with a traditional wooden racket and has tried a modern, high-tech version knows what has changed. Today's large, light rackets let even amateurs send the ball over the net more easily and with greater power.

The arms race in tennis began in earnest in 1977, when a double-strung racket, which employed two sets of strings that did not touch, hit the professional circuit. A plastic coating on the strings made them look like spaghetti, so the rackets were dubbed "spaghetti strung." The separated sheets of strings let the ball sit on the racket longer during a stroke, helping a player put considerably more topspin on the ball.

The invention unleashed a string of upsets that year. At the U.S. Open, Michael Fishbach, who was ranked 200th in the world, beat Stan Smith, who was seeded 16th. Georges Goven, a relatively unknown French player, beat the commanding Ilie Nastase at a tournament in Paris. Nastase quickly switched to a spaghetti-strung racket and defeated Guillermo Vilas, ending the latter's 50-match winning streak. Soon after, the International Tennis Federation banned spaghetti stringing.

Radar guns at international competitions have shown that other innovations in rackets and balls—in combination with athletic skills—continue to drive up serving speeds. The composite materials in rackets allow them to be lighter and cover a wider area yet withstand the tension of being tightly strung. The result is a bigger sweet spot for hitting hard, accurate shots and higher-velocity serves. A few pros, notably John McEnroe, have complained that the rackets threaten to transform tennis into a game of blistering serves that only incredible returners like Andre Agassi can handle. The technology improvements that bring more amateurs into the sport might destroy their interest in the professional game if matches turn into strings of one-shot points.

Banned Bats

For many Americans, one of the most obvious consequences of technology emerged in Little League baseball in the early 1970s, when the ping of aluminum bats started replacing the crack of wood. The metal bats provide an economic advantage because they don't break like wood ones do. But for the players, aluminum bats pack more punch. They are lighter, so a player, especially a child, can swing faster, sending out harder hits. And manufacturers can move an aluminum bat's center of gravity toward the knob, which also increases swing speed. Finally, the ball rebounds better off the aluminum, again adding power to the outgoing sphere. James A. Sherwood, director of the Baseball Research Center at the University of Massachusetts at Lowell, says, "The sad part is, it's like the technology is beginning to control the game more than the players' ability."

Aluminum bats never affected Major League Baseball, where they are banned. But they raised a ruckus in the National Collegiate Athletic Association. To protect fielders, NCAA officials want to prevent aluminum bats from hitting too hard. To do that, they turn to Sherwood. His facility includes a Baum Hitting Machine, in which motors collide a baseball and a bat at computer-controlled speeds. The device then measures the ball's rebound. In the past, an aluminum bat hit a ball about 10 miles an hour faster than a comparable wood bat did. The NCAA ruled recently that an allowable aluminum bat can hit a ball only as fast as a 34-inch, 31-ounce wood bat can. According to Sherwood's results, with a pitch speed of 70 miles an hour and a bat-tip speed of 85 mph, a ball takes off at about 96 mph.

Following suit, other organizations are also instituting similar rule changes. For instance, the National Federation of State High School Associations is developing a rule mandating that a 34-inch wood bat and a 34-inch aluminum bat hit the same. It is apparent, however, that manufacturers and players will continue to seek a technological edge. Perhaps manipulating a bat's center of gravity will create an advantage. "Here it's kind of technology versus technology," Sherwood adds. "I have the machine that can catch it, but they may find a way to circumvent the machine."

Laying Down the Law

The athletic arms race involves many factions. Players want better performance. Professional team owners and college recruiters crave improved records to attract more fans and make more money. Manufacturers pursue bigger market share by producing "better" products. It is therefore up to governing bodies to limit technological advances enough to preserve a sport's integrity. The question is how best to do that. Some officials confront advances one by one, writing a new rule to outlaw each specific device. Market researcher Gelberg, however, thinks that rules should protect specific skills. The USGA's symmetry rule is a good example: it outlaws any ball—not just the Polara—that performs in a certain way. Experts such as Sherwood and Dryden are helping baseball and hockey in their pursuits of equally useful rule changes.

If governing bodies take on technology case by case, it will leave them constantly open to new attacks. "The problem with ad hoc design standards is that you're going to get a new design tomorrow that will have the same impact on the game, the same impact on challenge, and it's going to be permitted because that particular design was not banned," Gelberg warns. She says defending skills, rather than limiting individual innovations, is the way to go.

Scientific American Presents: Building the Elite Athlete, Fall 2000

The Unblinking Eye

Technologies that can see better than humans encounter a mixed reception on the playing field

BRUCE SCHECHTER

Fans of sports and magic know that the hand is often quicker than the eye. Just ask Vinny Testaverde. In 1998 Testaverde, the New York Jets' quarterback, had brought his team to within striking distance of beating the Seattle Seahawks in one of the final games of the season. On fourth down, with 20 seconds left in the game and the ball on the Seahawks' five-yard line, the Jets needed a touchdown for victory. Testaverde carried those last five yards himself and was tackled just as he dove across the goal line. Head linesman Earnie Frantz signaled a touchdown, and Jets fans went wild.

It was a classic football moment—except for one detail. The referee was wrong. The videotape replay and newspaper photographs clearly showed that Testaverde went down before he ever crossed the goal line. For football fans it was the final straw. The Jets' unearned victory was the most egregious illustration of the occasional and unavoidable fallibility of human officials. Earlier that season the Buffalo Bills had been the victims of a couple of botched calls in a loss to the New England Patriots—and their owner was fined $50,000 for complaining. Officials had even managed to foul up a coin toss in a game on Thanksgiving. These highly publicized mistakes finally forced league officials and team owners to reinstitute the use of instant replays by officials, something they had been resisting for seven years.

Sports fans and athletes have always been critical, to say the least, of the impartiality and visual acuity of the umpires, referees, linesmen and others who are charged with making sure the rules of sport are observed. Until the 1960s, differences of opinion were simply that—fans and officials had to agree to disagree. Whether a pitch was over the plate or a foot was over the line was a fact writ in water. Then Roone Arledge of ABC Sports began to experiment with new video technology and radically reshaped the experience of viewing sports. He liberated sports from time.

Arledge employed cameras to isolate and analyze, putting them in places they had never been before: on the sidelines, in the end zone, on cranes and even underwater. He also used the ability of videotape to freeze a moment or play it back in slow motion, revealing in unprecedented detail "the thrill of victory and the agony of defeat." This technology has its roots in experiments conducted almost a century earlier by English photographer Eadweard Muybridge. Muybridge had used a series of still cameras to capture the gait of a horse and to resolve the controversy in racing circles over whether all four feet of a galloping horse are ever simultaneously off the ground (they are). Arledge's instant replays cleared up one question—referees do indeed make mistakes—but also triggered an endless string of squabbles over disputed plays.

Going Back to the Videotape

In 1986 the National Football League gave in to the increasing pressure from fans armed with proof of the fallibility of referees and began to use instant replay to help in disputed plays. Unfortunately, videotape technology was cumbersome and slow—it takes time to rewind and cue up a tape—and the camera angles sometimes made the replays hard to interpret. In 1991 a replay took over three minutes to review. In that season, 570 plays were examined, and 90 calls were reversed. League officials would later admit that of these at least nine were reversed incorrectly. It did not seem to the owners worth the trouble, time and expense. Besides, they reasoned, in the course of a season, mistakes should even out. So the NFL discontinued playbacks.

By 1998 it was evident that sometimes things do not even out. After the season of Testaverde's phantom touchdown, the owners voted to reinstate instant replay, an experiment that continues into the current season. In the intervening years, technology had caught up, making the process faster and easier to manage. Video could now be stored in computer memory, so no time was lost in rewinding. Cameras had gotten sharper. Still, replays took about two and a half minutes to review, so an elaborate set of rules was concocted to limit them: each team could demand only two replay challenges during a game (except in the final two minutes, when replays could be requested only by a "replay official"). If the replay showed that the field officials had made the right call, the challenging team would lose a time-out. So far the system has been judged to work well enough that it has been reinstituted for the 2000 season. The NFL is also considering other gadgets, such as the Scanz Scannor, a palm-size wireless device that can download and display video directly to those on the field, allowing the field-level officials instant access to replays.

Such technologies will undoubtedly change the way football and other sports are played. Taken to the extreme, they raise the specter of a future without human judgment calls. Although it is easy to imagine that technology will make such a future possible, it seems improbable that sports fans would entertain such an abrupt break with tradition. Still, the fallibility of human arbiters will very likely preserve a place for digital video cameras and computers. Many will welcome the veneer of scientific objectivity that technology brings to sports, but others will insist that this objectivity is an illusion. Just as juries may continue to doubt DNA evidence, sports officials will question the inter-pretation of replays.

As Cincinnati Bengals president Mike Brown said of football's instant replay, "It still has to be operated by people. [When] you get into decisions made by people, that can go awry." And technology can go awry as well. To err is human, it seems. When a machine makes an error, forgiveness is not only divine, it is nearly impossible. Nowhere is this better illustrated than in the sport of tennis.

When a tennis ball served by Pete Sampras or another top pro hits the court, it is traveling at approximately 100 miles an hour. The ball will stay in contact with the court for about four milliseconds before bouncing off at about 60 miles an hour. All this is taken in by an official who must render a decision. With action so fast, professional tennis matches employ as many as 11 officials to monitor the players, watch the boundaries and the net, and keep score. Using technology to replace some of these officials has most likely been motivated more by economics than by a desire for greater accuracy.

In 1979 a device known as Cyclops was introduced at Wimbledon to mon-itor the service line and to decide if serves are in or out. The system resembles a burglar alarm. Beams of infrared light are directed just beyond the line. When the ball interrupts the beam—as it must if the serve is long by a small margin—an alarm goes off. For the most part the system works well, but it does have blind spots, which have angered some already temperamental players. Balls that are hit very far out never cross Cyclops's glare and can therefore be judged in. More troubling, the carpet on indoor courts can shift and expand as the day heats up and the players run and slide. This means that whereas Cyclops's beams are unmoved, the court lines can shift by an inch or two, so a ball that the sys-tem judges in is actually out (or vice versa). But from the player's point of view perhaps the worst thing about Cyclops is that it just sits there, beeping imperturbably. They would agree with Boris Becker, who once remarked, "I would prefer linesmen doing the job, because I cannot talk to the Cyclops."

For better or worse, Cyclops seems to be here to stay, if for no other reason than that electronic officials are cheaper than humans. Attempts to eliminate the other linesmen have been less successful. One system, invented by an Australian company, involved mixing magnetic particles in with the rubber of the tennis ball. Wires embedded in the court sense the passing of these metallized balls and determine their position. Unfortunately, at some of its first outings the device, known as TEL (Tennis Electronic Lines), malfunctioned and emitted random beeps, which was too much for already oversensitive players to bear. TEL technology is still not a part of the professional tennis circuit.

Keep the Umpires

In general, tennis fans are fairly forgiving, preferring to leave tantrums over questionable decisions to players. Baseball fans exhibit no such restraint. Scorn for umpires is almost as much a part of baseball as hot dogs or the seventh-inning stretch. A pitch takes about half a second to travel from the pitcher's fingers to the catcher's glove, so it is not surprising that umpires occasionally confuse balls and strikes. What is surprising is that although the technology exists to capture the trajectory of the ball in flight and to render an inhumanly accurate verdict on exactly where it crossed the plate, nobody is clamoring to replace or even supplement human umpires with computers. Not yet.

The system in question, which is marketed under the name SuperVision, was first introduced in the early 1990s by QuesTec, a small company in Deer Park, N.Y. Two cameras, one located on the first-base line, the other on the third-base line, follow the pitch. The cameras are fast enough to take 16 pictures of the ball along the way. A computer program isolates the ball and uses triangulation to locate its position at each of the 16 points to within an inch. "We are working on bringing that down to a half an inch," says QuesTec's Mike Russo. Using these positions, the computer constructs a three-dimensional graphic of the trajectory that can be rotated and examined from any angle. SuperVision convinced any remaining skeptics that a curveball really does curve.

Baseball's adoption of the SuperVision system has been slow. As with any new technology, the first versions were expensive and balky. In 1996, for example, MSG Network in New York City gave SuperVision a spin. The commentators were impressed by its ability to distinguish curve from slider but were not equally wowed by its sense of pace. During one game, it declared that a ball that had left the pitcher's hand at 85 miles an hour arrived at the catcher's glove at the same speed. MSG announcer Jim Kaat turned to his producer and said, "I can't do this. A ball can't do that."

Russo claims that such problems are a thing of the past, eliminated by better software and hardware and by better-trained operators. Televised baseball games continue to make use of the technology. Still, this hidebound professional sport probably won't soon adopt SuperVision or any other system that replaces the umpires who call balls and strikes. Sport is about tradition as much as it is about competition. The reams of statistics so cherished by baseball fans testify to the powerful ties the game has to the past. Comparing today's players to the greats of seasons gone by adds a vital richness to a fan's appreciation. How could a perfect game pitched by David Wells and called by a human umpire ever truly be compared with the accomplishment of some future hurler whose strike zone was circumscribed by a machine? When a catcher fools the umpire into calling an outside pitch a strike, he is being no more dishonest than a runner stealing a base—a certain amount of guile is built into the game. Fooling a computer is not as easy, which makes it unlikely that one will be seen on the field anytime soon.

Off the field, however, technologies like SuperVision are quickly becoming part of the fan's experience of sports. "Everything we do in terms of technology is to embellish the broadcast of the game in the form of storytelling," says Arthur Smith, executive vice president of programming and production for Fox Sports Networks. Smith uses SuperVision, along with technologies such as robotic cameras and telestrators, which allow commentators to draw directly on the screen, to enhance the coverage of a game. "With us it's always about trying to make the game more interesting. It's not how sophisticated a technology is, it's how you use it."

The designers of new arenas and stadiums are beginning to pay as much attention to data lines as to sight lines. Baseball fans sitting in a few hundred expensive seats at Tropicana Field, home of the Tampa Bay Devil Rays, or at Qualcomm Stadium, where the San Diego Padres play, can take advantage of ChoiceSeats, a computer system that floods them with information on the game.

Each ChoiceSeat is equipped with flat-panel touch screens from which computer-literate fans can call up instant replays from half a dozen camera angles or peruse player statistics. They can order food from the snack bar, play computer games or even go shopping for merchandise on the Internet. The game on the field just a few feet away could become little more than a distant, bright, three-dimensional display. But if we are lucky, the computer won't interfere with the pure enjoyment of watching the game, nor will it change the way baseball is played. So, for the immediate future, the umpire will remain a bum.

*Scientific American Presents: Building the Elite Athlete, Fall 2000
Further Information: An explanation of how SuperVision works can be found at www.questec.com on the World Wide Web.*

INDEX

Italicized page references indicate illustrations. Figures are indicated with a lower case "f" following the page number.

bulimia, 19

bulking up (hypertrophy), 30–32, 37–39, 45–48

Buller, A. J., 47

bumetanide, 69

caffeine, 68

carbon isotope ratio (CIR) test, 74, 99–101

cardiac muscles, 24, 31, 84

Carpenter, William, 116

Carson, James, 38

Catlin, Don H.
    drug testing and diuretic use, 71
    on drug testing research financing, 81
    on drug use and ethics, 61
    testosterone testing, 99–100, 101
    THG identification, 96–97, 98

cattle, and gene therapy, 90

Caucasian athletes, and testosterone levels, 66

Center for Research and Education in Special Environments (CRESE), 154

CFD (computational fluid dynamics) software, 134, 153

cheating, 62–67, 70

chemicals, performance-enhancing. *See* drugs, banned; steroids, anabolic

chlorthalidone, 69

ChoiceSeats, 173

choking, 110

chorionic gonadotropin (hCG), 69

Cincinnati Sportsmedicine and Orthopaedic Center, 14, 16

CIR (carbon isotope ratio) test, 74, 99–101

clap skate, 6, 157–58

the Claw, 149

clenbuterol, 68

climbing, free solo, 126–27

clothing. *See* apparel

competition, 105–6

computational fluid dynamics (CFD) software, 134, 153

computer programs, 134, 153, 172–73

Condron, Bob, 70

confidence, 115, 116, 117–18

Connolly, Pat, 64

Coombs, Doug, 127

Counsilman, James "Doc," 133–34, 135–36

Court of Arbitration for Sport, 67, 75, 138

creatine, 34

creatine monohydrate, 22

Hanzliková, Véra, 31

Harvard University, 87

Hawk, Tony, 139, 145–46

Hayes, John, 2, 99, 100

hCG (chorionic gonadotropin), 69

Head Sport, 149, 151

heart muscle tissue, 23

Held, Dick, 162

Hermansson, Gunnar, 66, 79

Hewett, Timothy E., 16

hGH (human growth hormone), 61, 65–66, 69, 74–75, 77–81

high jumping, 4–5

high-resolution mass spectrometer (HRMS), 73

hiking boots, 149

hockey, 159–60

Hohn, Uwe, 162

Holmstrom, Fred, 160

home-court advantage, 107–8

"Hoop City," 10

hormone replacement therapy (HRT), 21

hormones
    ACL injuries and, 17–18
    cloning, 23–24, 38–39
    energy deficits and, 19
    human growth hormone (hGH), 61, 65–66, 69, 74–75, 77–81
    muscle building, 63, 66

sex, and transcription, 37

synthetic (*see* erythoropoietin, synthetic (EPO); testosterone, synthetic)

Howe, John, 149

HRMS (high-resolution mass spectrometer), 73

HRT (hormone replacement therapy), 21

human growth hormone (hGH), 61, 65–66, 69, 74–75, 77–81

hydrochlorothiazide, 69

hypertrophy (bulking up), 31–32, 37–39, 45–48, 54

hypnotherapy, 104

ice skating, 145

ideomotor (Carpenter) effect, 116

IFs (International Federations), 67, 70, 75

IGF-I (insulinlike growth factor-I), 38, 87–88

imagery training (visualization), 111–12, 115–17

"in the groove," 108–11

injuries
    breasts and, 137
    female athlete triad and, 19–21
    gender comparisons, 11–12, 11f, 13–14, *15*, 16–18

National Collegiate Athletic Association (NCAA), 164

National Federation of State High School Associations, 165

National Football League, 168

National Hockey League, 159

National Institute of Arthritis and Musculoskeletal and Skin Diseases, 13

National Off-Road Bicycle Association, 128

National Olympic Committees (NOCs), 67, 70–71, 75

NCAA (National Collegiate Athletic Association), 164

Neely, Bob, 128

Nepela, Daniel, 160

neurotransmitters, 123–24

The New Skiing Mechanics (Howe), 149

Newton's theory of gravity, 133, 135

New York Jets, 167

Nike, 155

"900" (skateboard maneuver), 139, 145–46

19-norandrostenediol, 68

19-norandrostenedione, 68

NOCs (National Olympic Committees), 67, 70–71, 75

norepinephrine, 124

Norwood, Scott, 106

Noyes, Frank R., 16–18

nutrition, 3, 19

officials, game, 167–70

the Ollie (skateboard maneuver), 140–41

Olympic Games
    biomechanic innovations at, 4
    drug labs at, 63
    drug testing and, 62–66, 70, 72–74
    "hGH Games," 65, 74
    world records at, 2, 157, 158

Olympic Laboratory (University of California Los Angeles), 99

Osman, Dan, 127

osteoporosis, 12, 19

Overland, Kevin, 157

ovulation, 18

Owens, Jesse, 6

pain tolerance, 118

parachuting, extreme, 128

patellofemoral syndrome, 13–14

Pendergast, David, 154

peptid hormones, 69. *See also* erythoropoietin, synthetic (EPO)

performance
    defining, vi

factors improving, 2–3, vi–vii
improvement statistics, 7f
limitation studies, 8–9
sports psychology and, 103–5
substances enhancing, 60–64 (*see
also specific names of substances*)
Perkins, Kieren, 138
personality, and performance, 104–5
Petersen, Trevor, 127
Petranoff, Tom, 162
PGA Victor, 160–61
Phelps, Jake, 146
Phelps, Michael, 153
Phillips, Bill, 33
photography, 168, 172–73
physics, 4, 8, 133–36, 139–47
physiological arousal, and performance, 107
Piedmontese cattle, 90
piezoelectric fibers, 148–51, *150–51*
Pittenger, Baaron, 71
playbacks, 167–73
plyometrics, 3
Polara, 160
pole vaulting, 6
Pope, Harrison G., Jr., 35–36
Pound, Richard W., 75–76
Price, Joan, 71
probenecid, 69, 71
progesterone, 17

prohormones, 34
propranolol, 69
protein supplements, 34
pseudoephedrine, 68
psychology, sports
assessment and evidence
supporting, 104–5, 112–13
associations for, 115
extreme sports and, 122–25
history of, 105
probability vs. streaks, 108–11
self-help techniques, 103–4,
111–12, 114–20
variables affecting performance,
105–8
Psychology Today, 22
pumping, 144
Pumping Iron (motion picture), 22
Purcell, Ed, 111
Pursley, Dennis, 138
Putukian, Margot, 20–21

QuesTec, 171–72
Quick, Richard, 132
Quintero, Patrice, 128

Raglin, John S., 8–9
records, athletic, 1, 2, 157, 158
referees and officials, 167–70
relaxin, 18

Vilas, Guillermo, 163

visualization, 111–12, 115–17

WADA (World Anti-Doping
    Agency), 75–76, 80, 83
Wallace, Gordon, 137
Watson, Jake, 129
Way, Danny, 144
weight lifting, 33–34, 35–36
weight training, 22, 23, 33, 35
Wells, David, 172
West, Jerry, 106
Wickersham Wall, Mount
    McKinley, 127
Williamson, Jed, 126
Wilson, Jean D., 97, 98
Wojtys, Edward M., 11, 12, 14, 18

women
    ACL injuries and, 10–17, 11f, 15
    female athlete triad, 12, 19–21
    self-image disorders of, 19, 35
The Women's Sports Medicine
    Center, 13
Woods, Tiger, 117
World Anti-Doping Agency
    (WADA), 75–76, 80, 83
World Series, 107–8

yams, wild, 100
Yessis, Michael, 3–4
Yosemite National Park, 126, 127

Zirngibl, Werner, 149

ABOUT THE AUTHORS*

Jesper L. Andersen works with Peter Schjerling and Bengt Saltin at the Copenhagen Muscle Research Center, which is affiliated with the University of Copenhagen and the city's University Hospital. Andersen is a researcher in the department of molecular muscle biology and a former coach of the sprint team of the Danish national track-and-field team.

Steven Ashley is a *Scientific American* technology writer and editor.

Steve J. Ayan is an editor at Gehirn & Geist.

Delia K. Cabe is a science writer who lives in Belmont, Massachusetts.

Mark Fischetti is an editor at *Scientific American*.

Marguerite Holloway is a contributing editor at *Scientific American*.

Mike May is a freelance writer based in Clinton, Connecticut.

Bengt Saltin works with Peter Schjerling and Jesper L. Andersen at the Copenhagen Muscle Research Center. He is director of the center, graduated from the Karolinska Institute in Stockholm in 1964 and worked as a professor of human physiology there and at the University of Copenhagen's August Krogh Institute. A former competitive runner, he has also coached the Danish national orienteering team.

Bruce Schechter is a freelance science writer and book author based in Brooklyn, N.Y., and the author of *My Brain Is Open: The Mathematical Journeys of Paul Erdös* (Touchstone Books, 2000).

Peter Schjerling works with Jesper L. Andersen and Bengt Saltin at the Copenhagen Muscle Research Center. Schjerling, a geneticist in the department of molecular muscle biology, recently changed his area of specialty from yeast to a considerably more muscular creature, Homo sapiens.

Michael Shermer writes the "Skeptic" column in *Scientific American*.

Sarah Simpson is a freelance writer who frequently contributes to *Scientific American*.

Gary Stix is an editor and writer for *Scientific American*.

H. Lee Sweeney is professor and chairman of physiology at the University of Pennsylvania School of Medicine. He is a member of the Board of Scientific Councilors for the National Institute of Arthritis and Musculoskeletal Diseases, scientific director for Parent Project Muscular Dystrophy, and a member of the Muscular Dystrophy Association's Translational Research Advisory Council. His research ranges from basic investigation of structures that allow cells to move and generate force, particularly the myosin family of molecular motors, to translating insights about muscle cell design and behavior into gene therapy interventions for diseases, including Duchenne muscular dystrophy. He took part in a 2002 symposium on the prospect of gene doping organized by the World Anti-Doping Agency.

Pearl Tesler is a science writer at the Exploratorium museum in San Francisco.

Frank Vizard is co-author of *The 21st Century Soldier*.

Glenn Zorpette is a former *Scientific American* editor.

*This information was compiled at the time the articles were originally published by *Scientific American*; some biographies may not be completely up to date.